T0065389

A Bid for
Eternity

Welcome to God's Auction House!

Tina Wash

WESTBOW
P R E S S®
A DIVISION OF THOMAS NELSON
& ZONDERVAN

Copyright © 2021 Tina Wash.

All rights reserved. No part of this book may be used or reproduced by
any means, graphic, electronic, or mechanical, including photocopying,
recording, taping or by any information storage retrieval system
without the written permission of the author except in the case
of brief quotations embodied in critical articles and reviews.

WestBow Press books may be ordered through booksellers or by contacting:

WestBow Press
A Division of Thomas Nelson & Zondervan
1663 Liberty Drive
Bloomington, IN 47403
www.westbowpress.com
844-714-3454

Because of the dynamic nature of the Internet, any web addresses or
links contained in this book may have changed since publication and
may no longer be valid. The views expressed in this work are solely those
of the author and do not necessarily reflect the views of the publisher,
and the publisher hereby disclaims any responsibility for them.

Any people depicted in stock imagery provided by Getty Images are models,
and such images are being used for illustrative purposes only.
Certain stock imagery © Getty Images.

ISBN: 978-1-6642-2005-8 (sc)
ISBN: 978-1-6642-2004-1 (e)

Print information available on the last page.

WestBow Press rev. date: 01/30/2021

Scripture quotations marked (NIV) are taken from the Holy Bible, New International Version®, NIV®. Copyright © 1973, 1978, 1984, 2011 by Biblica, Inc.® Used by permission of Zondervan. All rights reserved worldwide. www.zondervan.com The "NIV" and "New International Version" are trademarks registered in the United States Patent and Trademark Office by Biblica, Inc.®

Scripture quotations marked (ESV) are from The ESV® Bible (The Holy Bible, English Standard Version®), copyright © 2001 by Crossway, a publishing ministry of Good News Publishers. Used by permission. All rights reserved.

Scripture quotations marked (NLT) are taken from the Holy Bible, New Living Translation, copyright ©1996, 2004, 2015 by Tyndale House Foundation. Used by permission of Tyndale House Publishers, Carol Stream, Illinois 60188. All rights reserved.

Scripture marked (KJV) taken from the King James Version of the Bible.

Scripture quotations marked (NRS) are from New Revised Standard Version Bible, copyright © 1989 National Council of the Churches of Christ in the United States of America. Used by permission. All rights reserved worldwide.

A Bid for Eternity

*"As the Father loved me, I also have
loved you; abide in my love.
If you keep My Commandments, you will abide in My love,
just as I have kept My Father's Commandments
and abide in His love."*

John 15:9 KJV

Preface

Life is given to us each day to do with as we choose. And, while God allows those choices, He is always offering encouragement to turn to Him for guidance - loving guidance, grace and mercy, as well as insight that is often beyond human understanding. It is when we respect and choose His plans for our lives that choices can be made with wisdom and understanding.

A Bid for Eternity is my effort to share some of the excitement and gratitude that a life with God will provide. Ideas provided are lessons learned through a lifetime of sometimes slow understanding of reality and the timely wisdom found in scripture that have allowed me to live that excitement and understand the gift of it. I am daily amazed how scripture that was written so long ago is still relevant and eye-opening to our lives today.

I am grateful that people in our Bible are examples of wise – and poor – choices just like the decisions we make today. It is not because I want to use their examples as any form of excuse for mistakes on my part. It is because the loving God was ALWAYS present to lead them and forgive them and to teach them and to simply love them because He wanted to.

Because He wanted to.

We are not called to simply exist. We are called to a loving relationship with Him. An exciting one! We also have a responsibility, as well as a privilege, to learn and grow each day of our lives. We are encouraged in so many ways to look for God in the midst of our days, to allow Him to guide and teach us as we live our lives. I realized that God had a plan for my life when a teenager. I have made mistakes, but God has always pointed out that His way will always be better and welcomed me with open arms. That is who He is; none of us deserve that. Yet, it is given freely in ways we need to be aware of.

The absolutely critical point I want you, the reader, to understand is that I do not know what additional blessings I would have experienced without those detours, but I do know the lessons God taught me on each and every one. Those mistakes have made me who I am so that I might share His love with others. And I am grateful beyond words.

Just as you may have made excuses in your spiritual life, I did too. It is my goal to help you see how the seemingly innocent words of "if" and "if only" can rob one of God's opportunities in each life.

It is my goal to let you feel the wonder of all that God has already provided for your 'life beyond amazing' and remind you that all are available when the time is right. They simply require that personal relationship that allows you to understand their importance and the need for gratitude in advance.

And most of all I hope you will choose a life of gratitude for all you have been offered. Saying "Thank You, Lord!"

should roll off your tongue naturally, consistently, and with heartfelt meaning.

Ever the teacher, may I encourage you to do three additional things?

1. Keep your Bible nearby as you read so that you too can experience the words of wisdom for yourself! Schedule a time later to read the verses in the context of the full lessons and experiences, and then return to the individual verses provided to remember their application to your own life.

2. Do not let familiar vocabulary keep you from understanding the deeper, insightful wisdom in some of the Bible verse vocabulary. You have the time for understanding, and no one can tell you otherwise.

3. And finally, if you are comfortable with it grab a pen and paper and write out your understanding and application of scripture and materials contained with this book.

No, dear reader, I am not asking for an essay. (I am always amazed when someone asks if he or she will be graded on their writing!). No one will grade your punctuation or misspelled words. No one will see your writing – it will be between you and God. It will be reminders that may someday allow you to share your God-given and God-blessed life with others.

Say your prayers. And spend your day
in God's Auction House!
Oh, the treasures that await you…

Contents

SECTION TWO

SECTION THREE

SECTION ONE

1

A Bid for Eternity

Welcome to God's Auction House!

To **bid** is to "offer (a certain price) for
something, especially at an auction."

Oxford dictionary

It is "an Authoritative direction or instruction."
It is "to Ask or Request earnestly to make
a serious effort to attain something."

The Free dictionary.

A bid is made by offering something currently
owned in exchange for something desirable.

Imagine the world's most glamorous wonderland of an
auction house filled with everything you seek…and all for
just one price. As you walk among the items you are filled
with wonder and anticipation; your heart and your mind

begin to realize that you have the opportunity to realize your dreams, your desires and your needs without fear of credit card bills and overdue payments.

As you continue to browse the tables laden with treasures you begin to notice that each item is more beautiful, more perfect than anything you now possess, and each has unbelievably been crafted, designed, and purposed just for you.

Immediately you make your way to the front of the room, ready to place your first bid – only to find this is an auction unlike any other. It may seem confusing at first, but after a few deep breaths you begin to understand.

The bid for each glorious item is the following: your life – not the loss of your life but the exchange of elements you already have: your trust, your faith, your pride, your time, your love, all given in exchange for gifts greater than you can imagine! Please note the word "exchange."

Each and every item is yours for the asking. It only requires your **choice** to accept each offering, to enjoy, to treasure, to recognize the value of each one. The price has already been paid – your presence is all the Auctioneer is waiting for.

A bid in this setting is no gamble, no bet in a poker game, no sacrifice any greater than the one already made by the Auctioneer. His name is Jesus, and He has been waiting for your arrival!

His Father, the owner of the auction house, has considered carefully all the items and reserved this special section just for you. That area is for a private auction – it was created and filled with treasure just for you. It may contain something others cannot see; it may contain a few surprises, because the items have been uniquely collected to guide you on your journey throughout life. This special collection contains all you will ever need, all you will ever truly want, and all the wonderful gifts God has in store for you – many of which you have never dreamed of!

All you must do is choose to participate in the auction of a lifetime. Choose to be blessed; to be forgiven; to be protected; to be loved, and to be amazed by the quality, joy and peace of each item offered. Choose to give up your old "trade-in" that is battered, broken, imperfect, and weak for that which IS perfect and perfectly given by the God of the Universe.

Will you choose to stay for an auction
unlike any you have ever attended?
Are you willing to recognize the value
of each and every item?
Are you excited? Oh, I hope so!

As you are ushered to your special section a guide regales you with stories of the provenance of a few of the items. It is important you understand each has had only one owner previously. Each item has been authenticated and the date of its creation established. The provenance of each item has significantly impacted the value of each and every item available – a value that is often beyond human understanding. Your Guide talks of works of fine art: Nature created with care and wisdom to provide you with physical needs as well as beauty to behold. And then, amazingly He reminds you that one specific area is devoted to letting you see the finest of the art: you, just as God created you to be.

In this section you will note there are original manuscripts seemingly written just for you. The most important one? Your Bible! Your guide reminds you there is always time to enjoy it.

Wait, can you hear it? There is music written by the greatest composers, playing live. Can it be? It sounds like choirs of angels in tune with those heavenly chords. Major keys that elevate our soul vs Minor keys for the drama, difficulty, uncertainties of life. Yet, all are sung by those who know how the songs will end.

Turn the corner and you enter the section reserved specifically for tools used in construction and yes, those well-used tools for repair. Engraved on one handle: *"Train up a child in the way he should go."* Proverbs 22:6 ESV. On another you find: *"Unless the Lord builds the house its builders labor in vain."* Psalm 127:1 ESV. The plaque on the far wall reads, *"…the Builder of a house has greater honor than the house itself. For every house is built by someone, but God is the builder of everything."* Hebrews 3:3-4 NIV. Take some time to read the full text of Hebrews, Chapter 3. Every tool in this auction house serves as a reminder of those roller coaster rides of life. Sometimes hard to reach the top, but the pause at the top to experience the reward is *breathtaking.* If not careful, however, that pause at the top can be short-lived when we lose sight of the one who helped us make the climb. If so, that pause will only last a moment and is sure to be followed by that literal *breath-taking* plummet to the bottom again. Perhaps the tools used for repair are more familiar; but your guide is sure to remind you that ALL the tools can be used when needed and will certainly make you stronger, regardless.

As you contemplate all that lies before you there is a gentle nudge from your guide. The tour is not complete. He pulls out a key and places it in your hand as he points to a door you passed on the way in but did not "actually" notice. Nearing it you begin to see its beauty, and your spirit begins to soar. The door is encrusted with pearls, one that shines even more brightly. Surely this must be the pearl of great price - truly this is the best item up for auction! It must be! Do you try your key in the lock or simply stand before it?

Matthew 13:44-45 is Jesus' parable of the hidden treasure in a field. The man was not looking for treasure – you didn't notice this door. Maybe he came upon it unaware, but he could not deny the beauty of it - you also missed the door but with help from your guide you find yourself unable to deny the beauty of this door. The man soon realized that while the field was not his, the treasure contained was worth any sacrifice so that he would not, could not lose a treasure far more valuable than anything he knew or owned or had even known he wanted! Will you try your key in the lock?

This final room on our tour of the auction house reminds us that near the construction tools and the tools worn by many repairs we can find something very, very special. It may be found by accident; we may have overlooked it; but once found we cannot help but know we have been blessed. Blessed not only by the treasure and the beauty of a pearl of great price but by the Owner and Auctioneer and our Guide throughout. Everyone and everything you will ever need has been gathered here just for you. And, all are simply waiting for the bidding to begin.

2

—⟨⟨⟨∘∅∘⟩⟩⟩—

Return to the Auctioneer

Hear His Stories and see the warmth in His smile

*"Sing to the Lord a **new** song;*
sing to the Lord all the earth."
Psalm 96:1 ESV

This is the "Day which the Lord Hath Made." Psalm 118:24
KJV. You are here for a reason;

you have been shown great wonders and have seen
confirmation of God's Great Love.

Let the Praises Begin! Say 'Thank you' for each and every
item put on reserve for you. You may never fully understand
their value, but you can trust the items are here for your
protection and joy and understanding. Acknowledge that
many would be impossible without God and without Jesus.
Express your awareness of the Trust required in a several of
the objects, but also admit your Understanding that nothing
will ever destroy you as long as you choose to have God by
your side.

It is almost time to begin the Bidding but a few things first…

Notice Psalm 96:1 ESV at the top of the page. "Sing to the Lord a new song." The *Quest Study Bible* poses a question for thought: "What's wrong with the old songs?" They are often more familiar, but does familiar necessarily mean better? They may or may not be enough for today's challenges. Those same words we recite without thinking, the same routines we live without really living, the same struggles we seem to repeat - are they enough? Each and every item on reserve in this auction house was selected to allow you to sing with joy. Psalm 96:1 looks for a "new song," one with developing maturity, gratitude for the mercy, greater understanding, and certainly a new song with clarity that we cannot make it through our days without help from on high. We need to realize it is important to keep our praises fresh, timely, and current. Today is physically and spiritually Day One of the rest of your God-given life. And oh, what a gift that is!

Existence is part of the past. Life is lived in the present.

Today, you have an auction to attend!

Today's tour, and each subsequent day of your life, is given to you, to do with as you wish. Choose to believe God's promises. Choose to accept Jesus' sacrifice on the Cross with you in mind long before you entered God's auction house. Choose to praise them first and last. Recognize and be grateful He "will never leave you nor forsake you." Hebrews 13:5 KJV. Or don't. Take the credit for the moments you survive, or ignore Who held your hand through difficulty…

and continue singing the same song, second verse, or is it the 10,000th verse?

Choose the better path. Enter your time with Jesus the Auctioneer and feel the love. See the look in His eyes as He continues to gaze upon one He has loved for so long. It is obvious there is no question that He realizes the sacrifice on the Cross was not in vain. Enjoy the childlike wonder of hearing His stories, of seeing the warmth in His smile. It is time to let him know you are grateful. It is an opportunity for you to say 'Thank you and I love you' face-to-face. You have certainly been blessed.

Never consider any past praise complete without need for additional gratitude, recognition of His mercy, and power, and love and understanding, and grace, and encouragement, and forgiveness and wisdom…how many more could you add to that list if you only took a moment right now to consider who Jesus is? Singing a new song to the Lord is just that – recognizing each new and generous gift He provides on a daily basis.

Personal note: I love the idea that He has already provided all we will ever need or want in advance. Can you just imagine what it would be like to really walk through that room reserved just for you and your future? I suppose in the midst of excitement there might also be a little fear about a few things, but that is why God reveals His Plans to us a little at a time. Every day He hears your voice and feels your love He looks into your room to see what is needed that day. Understanding and recognizing that should lead to gratitude and praise for who God is on a daily basis as well.

God is prepared; therefore, you are prepared.

Start singing that joyful tune. Lamentations 3:22-23 ESV says, "*The steadfast love of the Lord never ceases; **His mercies** never come to an end; they are new every morning…*" The question begging to be asked is, do we discount that fact? *One*, you woke up – even on a bad day that one fact truly is hope illustrated. *Two*, there will always be someone to greet you with love and hope for the new day. He is God, and I can confidently say He has "plans not to harm you but to give you a future and a hope." Jeremiah 29:11 NIV. *Three*, the God of the Universe is looking forward to sitting down with you and discussing the day ahead; He is anxious to tell you stories of men and women in the Bible who experienced many of the same events you have or will encounter. He has words of affirmation, comfort, encouragement and words of love to fill you with joy as you enter a day of responsibility. It is a privilege to spend time with the One who provided those gifts, and who knows what surprises lay in store? *Four*, you get to enjoy that relationship with Him!

When I consider my own life, I am grateful, first and foremost for the blessings I had as a child: two incredible parents who never spoiled me with material things but loved me so much I never realized I was missing anything. They taught me and forgave me in equal measure. However, it has to be my choice as an adult to live by their example. The past is not enough to govern our lives today. It must be paired with all our Bible teaches. We have a responsibility as well as a privilege to learn and grow from those lessons daily. As hard as it is to sometimes admit, we do have more to learn, more to be grateful for, and we certainly have more mercy and blessings to be recognized. Choose to never overlook that in the midst of "life." It is so very important to our todays and our tomorrows.

The clock on the wall tells us the auction and the bidding are simply waiting to begin upon your arrival, but perhaps you might wish to spend a little more time with the Owner of that glorious auction house first. I can assure you He will make time in His schedule for you. Are you willing to exchange a portion of your time for the privilege of knowing more about God as well? If so, prepare yourself now for one of the best days ever!

Take a few minutes to compose yourself. Consider how it is that you are given such privilege. It was not earned; it is given. But it must not be entered into lightly.

Remember that each and every auction bid is an exchange of some part of your life for the wonders of God. Before we can ever attempt a commitment for the future God has planned for us, we must deal honestly with today. The present is not always seen as "Ideal." We cannot gloss over it with fond memories colored by rose-tinted glasses as we often do with the past – "the good old days." Today, you are tired. Bills need to be paid; work has to be done, and life has to be lived. Mistakes must be corrected. Sins must be confessed. Too many responsibilities to wear those rosy-tinted glasses today. You do have responsibilities, and life can quickly encourage us to forget that our first responsibility is to God.

In the midst of daily stress Prayer is often relegated to the "Land of Later." Forgotten is time with Him and the mercy He provides; remaining are our wishes for the big blessings that could make life easier...Money trees in the backyard, Energy and good health to accompany us on an adventure rather than a day of responsibility. We seek unconditional love from bosses, family, folks on the freeway, and ourselves as well. Life is forever changing and evolving into the life we are choosing. And God is ever waiting, providing that unconditional love and waiting for us to involve Him in that daily life.

Honestly ask yourself:

Are your actions choosing a life without God -
maybe not consciously or entirely,
but are you withholding the invitations that welcome Him
into every aspect of your life and not just a chosen few?

Are you ignoring the opportunities to hear His Voice
and see His presence throughout days of responsibility?

Are you suffering and longing for more to
life without taking necessary steps
to provide the joyous foundation of mercy
and love God offers each morning?

Are you willing to forget yesterday's trials and tribulations,
and begin each day praising God and
thanking Him for what is to come?

No more "same song, second verse" but rather:
New Mercies, New Perspective, New Joy,
New Recognition of God before taking on the world.
And New Praise for Him.

Choose a willingness to build a new and improved, stronger foundation in God.

Allow yourself to become open to a new awareness of just how deep the love of Jesus is.

Be ready to be amazed they could love you so very, very much!

Isn't that a great way to begin a day of responsibility? And, truthfully, isn't it a good way to close out the old ones?

3

―――∞∞∞―――

A Visit with the Owner
of the Auction House

Know God Know Yourself

"I praise you, for I am fearfully and wonderfully made…"
Psalm 139:14 ESV

Know your God; Know Yourself, and then, only then, will life make sense. Only then can you see yourself through the Owner's eyes. Whether you realize it or not you are the most important item – of any cost – in this grand auction house. It may seem you are the one viewing items that you would enjoy, but even a few moments with the Owner of this Auction House will make it clear He is looking at a treasure as well. He has been viewing one "item" He treasures greatly; He has been looking at you. Yes, God treasures you. Period.

Know how important you are to Him. Know the Bible speaks only truth, even about you! Over and over God illustrates how gifted, how lovable, how precious you are to God. Over and Over and Over. Allow yourself to see all you are, and all you can be. And, by the way, only then can you truly begin to enjoy the miracle that you are - the Miracle the Owner is gazing at so lovingly. The more you read your Bible the more obvious it becomes that your biblical self-worth can accomplish great and mighty things for God – you are strong and capable. You are never alone – God is always at your side. You possess unique gifts and abilities that God has provided and that will enable you to accomplish any task God leads you to. You are never isolated from God; He is only a thought away.

You are God's treasure, a child loved with a love that surpasses understanding. You may never be perfect, but you can be forgiven. And every characteristic you possess can impact the lives of those around you in life-changing ways, in ways that allow others to see the love and grace and sacrifice of Jesus as well. The question is: 'Are you willing to accept yourself?' Are you willing to recognize you possess the qualities the world is looking for? Are you willing to use your unique and wonderful life to glorify God and teach others?

Acceptance and Accountability

Self-acceptance, biblical or otherwise can be a struggle for many, and while life's regrets may come far too easily, the acceptance of who you are and who you were created to be tends to be a slow-moving adaption. True understanding and acceptance of all that God has already placed inside you may take time to comprehend. It is up to us to learn about

God's gifts and plans and willingness to guide us. Don't let your lack of understanding or acceptance become a regret as you look back on your life.

Do not confuse your identity based on environmental factors, education, physical characteristics, or even social standing, with your identity in God. On the surface it is easy to identify our likes and dislikes, our strengths and weaknesses, but God's gifts and plans are there, just below the surface waiting to be noticed. Will you place A Bid for Eternity? If so, I can guarantee many of God's gifts are already within you. They have been safely planted inside you so that no one can take them from you, and each gift stands ready to help you be the person God will ask to join Him in joy, in peace, in His plans for good. All you have to do is start the conversation with God, refresh the relationship with Jesus, and choose the courage to simply believe God's truth.

Knowing you and God together have the capability to change the word in small, or even greater ways can still create insecurity or doubt, or it can lead to excitement, purpose and gratitude for the One who makes it possible. Knowing you have the chance, responsibility and privilege to change the world for greater good ought to be enticing, sobering, or at least humbling. Knowing God allowed His own Son to be crucified on a cross to insure you never have to lose the person He created you to be. No evil can destroy you unless you let it. Believe that. Let it encourage you to seek the only One who can use your life in miraculous ways.

You were created for a purpose greater and higher than anything you can dream of. You were created for a purpose more wonderful than any societal expectation - a purpose of truly making a difference – a good and needed difference. That purpose is a life-giving, peace enduring, and a grace led life that can only exist because God loves you, and Jesus made that second chance, that fresh start possible.

You are a teacher by your actions.

You are an encourager by your words.

You are a healer of broken spirits by your love.

You are an example of one who fails at times but rises again to move forward in grace given freely by your Father in Heaven.

You are a scholar – if you choose to learn more about God's day-to-day interaction with mankind as detailed just for us in the Bible.

You were created for joy, for yourself but also for God's joy in seeing you grow and prosper and mature in love, both for yourself and to share with others.

You were created because you are important. Know that the Bible speaks only truth, even about you! Over and over God illustrates how gifted, how lovable, how precious you are to Him. Over and over and over. The more you read, it becomes obvious that your biblical self-worth can accomplish great and mighty things for God – you are strong and capable. You are never alone – God is always at your side. You possess unique gifts and abilities that enable you to accomplish any task God leads you to. You are never isolated from God; He is only a thought away. You are God's treasure, a child loved with a love that surpasses understanding. You may never be perfect, but you are forgiven. And every characteristic you possess can impact the lives of those around you in life-changing ways, in ways that allow others to see the love and grace and sacrifice of Jesus as well. The question is are you willing to accept yourself? Are you willing to recognize you possess the qualities the world is looking for? Are you willing to use your unique and wonderful life to glorify God, live a life of purpose, and as a result, be an example for others?

One caveat that probably should be mentioned…the closer you get to believing all God is and all you are and all the both of you are capable of, the more you may become a target of doubt or insecurity or dare we say, laziness. It happens to the best of us. Choose not to be afraid; take your concerns, doubts, any negative emotions quickly to God. Be honest about what you are feeling and then be determined to stay nearby and listen as God presents His reassurance and His willingness to defend you against any fiery dart that comes your way. That battle is God's and the victory has already been won. All you are experiencing is only worn-out reruns that have lost their power to even entertain because you already know the ending.

If you are like so many others this is about the time you begin asking about specifics of the Plan. Human nature, even if filled with faith, still wants to know the full plan. Not knowing and still trusting may require reassurance that can be found in scripture and prayerful conversations with the Owner. Are you willing to seek that knowledge, that confidence, that opportunity to understand? Has God made a plan for good and not to harm? Jeremiah 29:11NIV says He did. "For I know the plans I have for you," declares the Lord, "plans to prosper you and not to harm you, plans to give you hope and a future." And you are invited to be a part of those plans. If you refuse, will or can God's plans be realized regardless of your choice? Yes, because God cannot and will not fail, but we will lose the opportunity to be a part of something outstanding. And that, my friend is the true definition of great loss.

4

Choices, Choices, Choices

Every morning, at precisely the same time a devotion arrives through an App, and regardless of whether I oversleep or delay giving it my attention for some "tyranny of the urgent" reason – the wisdom will remain until I choose to read it. Today's wisdom was based on Jeremiah 15:16 and my application of that wisdom took me through many a bakery this afternoon, literally and figuratively...

> *When your words came, I ate them; they*
> *were my joy and my heart's delight,*
> *For I bear Your Name, Lord God*
> *Almighty."* Jeremiah 15:16 NIV

My first thought was to pause at the words "I ate them." Eating words written in ink, on paper with no verifiable origin - not sure that is healthy. Then, I was reminded of Mother's words on Friday nights that included her trust I would behave regardless of where I was, or what I was doing. It was quickly followed by the warning: "Don't make my eat my words." But Jeremiah was talking about the desire for the words of God.

And in my typical, sometimes random, style of application of scripture I instantly thought of something I enjoy. I have no problem eating – but cake could probably be listed as one of my favorites. Will Rogers once said, "I have never met a man I did not like." Well, I have never tasted a cake I did not like. I will eat cake whenever it is available and enjoy it thoroughly. I will enjoy it regardless of the variety, because I see cake as a celebratory delight. And, despite the instant desire to buy a birthday cake and claim that somewhere someone is having a birthday, and it would be rude not to celebrate it with him or her, I am quickly reminded that it ought to be the same with reading my Bible and praying that two-way prayer that allows God to speak as well as listen to me.

Honestly, if I truly focus on the words God speaks and allow myself to see their application to my life the joy not only equals but surpasses the delight of any cake I have ever had.

Jeremiah's intent was to share his response to God's words; He chose to internalize them, savor them, enjoy them. Far too many are afraid to hear God speak much less internalize His message. Jeremiah was not. We have no reason to be afraid either.

Can you think of others in the Bible who treasured the words of God and Jesus that much? Jesus said, "Come, follow me; I will make you fishers of men," Matthew 4:19 NIV. The response: Peter and Andrew followed Jesus without questioning. Acts 9: 1-22 NIV says, Paul "fell to the ground" when he met Jesus on the Road to Damascus.

That is awe, humility and the impact of a life-changing event. On the Cross Jesus said, "Yet, not my will be done." Luke 22:42 ESV. That is true love for God and definitely sacrifice for those He came to save - you and me.

Noah built an ark, risked ridicule, lacked full understanding of God's plan but followed it anyway. (Genesis 6) Simply because God told him to. Gideon crawled out of the winepress to do that which God had commanded. By the way he was in the winepress, behind a 3-foot wall, trying to hide from God and the previous instruction given by God, Gideon's personal call to action - that same instruction Gideon had rejected out of fear. (Judges 6) Jonah learned a hard lesson in the belly of a whale. His sin was pride and fear of looking foolish when he knew God well enough to know that despite a scene declaring the sins of Nineveh would lead to total destruction, despite creating a scene to share God's plans for the hostile territory God would still forgive and save the people of Nineveh. It did take Jonah three days to reach humility in the presence of God's commands, but God's purpose was never defeated: the entire city of Nineveh was saved. (Jonah 1). Pause to consider three days in the belly of a great fish to admit a mistake! That is stubbornness.

The single motivating factor in those circumstances was the words of one whose Authority was unquestionable. Only with time spent in study can we begin to recognize God's presence and hear His voice minute-by-minute. Not only in your life but in the lives of others.

Only then can you begin to recognize all we have been given by grace – a grace so necessary, because we all have bits of Noah and Gideon and Jonah within us, not to mention

Eve and David and so many others. Look at the impact of their actions.

Would you be offended if I stopped to ask what you accomplished today? Immediate response might be "That is imagining my life today could begin to compare with those listed above, and that by the way, is absolutely ridiculous!" Reasonable response until you realize God has not changed. He was willing to help and empower those individuals, and so many more throughout time, and He has power left over to mold and strengthen you into a person who can accomplish great good, who can bless others, who can truly make a difference. We are living in a time we all need to take God's hand, follow His lead, and become the people He knows we can be.

He has the grace to allow us to become the people God knows we can be.

The key is you cannot know that straightforward offer of grace if you do not know Him. Or you won't listen to Him. Or if you think you have no time for Bible Study. Or if you think you do not have the proper words to pray. We are daily fed lies that keep us from God. And yet, we daily have opportunities to know more of God, and the more we know the more we can begin to recognize all the potential that lives within us, just waiting to be utilized. The more we know God the more we can understand all that He placed in each of us is simply waiting for the day we acknowledge it. Then we can begin to do those great and mighty things that will make this world a better place.

**Last, but never least, we will also have
the honor of seeing God glorified.**

One last comment – knowing that all you have heard from God is true… Knowing yourself just a little bit better the time has come for you to decide - for yourself - if His loving view of the person you are is the person you wish to be. If so, tell Him. If so, say thank You. If so, choose to enter the bidding with confidence, understanding and gratitude. God's blessings are overflowing!

And the Auctioneer is waiting!

5

The Plan

"For I know the plans I have for you" declares the Lord,
"plans to prosper you and not to harm you,
plans to give you hope and a future."
Jeremiah 29:11 NIV

As you leave the office of the Auction House Owner you experience a sudden wave of panic that just almost overwhelms. Truly, everything there is a treasure of greater value than you could ever understand throughout your lifetime. Everything you will ever need has been included, and all that you see can and will be a source of joy if you let it. Difficulties will arise, but there will still be joy in knowing how well prepared, how lovingly comforted, or simply how each and every event of your life can encourage your understanding of God.

And now you are beginning to see the need for a plan. Randomly wandering through and choosing that which is most beautiful or exciting may not meet the need for a life well-lived. Do not misunderstand – there will be beauty and excitement, but there will also be struggle and fear and loss.

**Items here have been chosen to insure
you never lose hope and
God never has to feel He has lost you.**

Our "struggle" often seems to lie in the fact that God doesn't always give us what we hope for; in truth, the struggle occurs because we don't know for sure what we should be hoping for.

Begin now to consider a plan that provides wisdom, hope, salvation, and trust. "Failing to plan is planning to fail." As I researched the familiar adage I found that credits had been given to a variety of authors, businessmen, and self-help gurus. Among names listed were Winston Churchill, Benjamin Franklin, and others. Variations of the adage have appeared in a multitude of forms over time. Posters even fill the hallways of high schools in an effort to encourage students to set their priorities with wisdom. And still, the message comes through with clarity: prepare now for the future.

**What you need is prayer before panic.
Always a wise first choice.**

Consider the effort put forth when one entertains a special guest or plans for a celebration of a special event such as a birthday, Thanksgiving or Christmas holidays. Now consider the celebration of the introduction of Jesus as the Messiah. John the Baptist announced Jesus' arrival by announcing, "This is He who was spoken of through the prophet Isaiah: 'a voice of one calling in the desert, Prepare the way for the Lord, make straight paths for Him." Matthew 3:3 NIV. It breaks my heart to know that too many ignore Jesus' presence, failing to understand that is what we should celebrate the most. Inviting Jesus into your life and your world is always a special event. Avoid any complicated song and dance routine that creates confusion. It is a simple choice – and one He is waiting for you to make. Create a favorable environment for Him; place no obstacles in your heart or your actions that will block His path. Do not insist Jesus' teachings and sacrifice compete with anything else for your time, your convictions, your choices; and certainly, do not insist Jesus compete with the world's ideas of a life well-lived. Therefore, realize you need to make a plan. Make a choice. Make a commitment and show the gratitude that is deserved.

Repeat: Make a Plan.

P   Praise God

"I will sing of Your strength;
I will sing aloud of your steadfast love in the morning."
Psalm 59:16 ESV

If that is the first step in your Plan the focus will move from you, your life, your problems to the One who knows how to restore your hope. That signifies not only your importance to God but His willingness to be nearby at all times; acknowledging that early saves a great deal of headaches. Ephesians 1:4 NIV says God "chose us in Him before the creation of the world to be holy and blameless in His sight … in accordance with His pleasure and will." Special note here: He chose us *before*; He *wanted* to do that. He is wise and already knew the end before the beginning. Yet, He still chose us despite our failures. Wouldn't it seem we should follow His example?

Let yourself remember those items from the auction that caused just a twinge of fear and realize God also has a plan. His includes Protection. His Plan began when He first presented you with a life of Purpose – a worthy journey throughout your life. He knows you can make a difference in this world and fully realizes that in any good endeavor, especially when the work is to bring glory to God and share the saving grace of Jesus, there will be opposition. Thus, He is already standing by to protect and reassure you. That alone could provide hope, yet there is so much more already in place to comfort, encourage and lead you. That is a fact. Therefore, begin your praise early, continue it throughout any endeavor, and when the finish line comes into view praise Him for the treasures along the way.

Isaiah 41:10 ESV says "So do not fear, for I am with you; do not be dismayed, for I am your God." Consider a few of your statements during a time of crisis. That verse was placed in your Bible just for the days you may say,

"I am afraid."
"I am losing hope and joy."
"I am unfocused, confused."

Note the differing perspective. You are speaking truth *as you know it*, but only one truth can change lives – God is in control; He will always provide hope if you are willing to listen, and He will always and forever be God. He cannot fail, therefore, when He chooses <u>you</u> to work for Him you cannot fail – unless you give up too soon.

P   **Praise God**
L   **Love God**

It is important to include the word "unconditionally" there, for both steps in the plan.

"Love the Lord your God with all thy heart, and with all thy soul, and with all thy mind, and with all thy strength." Mark 12:30 KJV. Remember, true love does not change its course or alter its effect when circumstances occur or "the wind changes direction." Love is eternal; if we follow His example, knowing the permanence of God's love, it becomes evident that love should not be given lightly. Love is not to be professed if it is false. Never attempt to mislead God or others by offering a poor version of love that is intended only to manipulate. Instead, see your example in Jesus who fully understands the deepest, most wonderful meaning of love - and the need for forgiveness rather than holding a grudge. Watch how quickly God forgives and then begins a rebuilding process that enables individuals to grow stronger and wiser. Experience the love that not only goes with you but also holds your hand when the way seems difficult.

That is important in your interaction with others and your interaction with God, and for God. Let me explain…if I asked if you loved God would you answer "yes?" However, if you are with others who deny God, condemn or show disrespect for God, does your love protect God? Do you speak up? Do you attempt to better explain who God is and let others know your choice to love God is the best part of your life? Or do you walk away to avoid controversy? I am not talking about theatrics here but about conviction that God is who He says He is. If you believe it, others can too, and they need to hear your voice. Others need to see proof that you believe what you say by showing God's type of love to others. There are many in this world who are in need of a kind heart that loves and wants the best for them regardless of the 'state' they may be in right now. Love sees reality but does not condemn.

Even on our best days we realize the confusion or frustration with varying religious views, conflict arising out of different nationalities, different skin tone, different political views and differing attitudes on lifestyles. That 'Can't we all just get along?' seems even more needed in today's world. May I make a respectful observation please? Conflict and confrontation certainly contain caustic comments and crisis, but prayer promises peace, patience, practical and positive solutions. (Like that alliteration there?) Yes, I am laughing as well as understanding that even those few moments spent creating that and time spent truly considering the meaning has a purpose. God is love, and He wants us to be a beacon of light and love for the world. That kind of love must also begin in your heart and then be spread to others. Note: that type of love can only exist when we recognize the power of prayer.

Love for God is not to be fickle – it is not to gain favor.
It is to show favor *for* God.
It may mean sacrifice; it may not.
Regardless of circumstances, it is needed.

You are one given the chance to show favor for God by spending time with Him minute by minute, day by day. Then, and only then, can you enter this world ready to let others see God's grace in you. God is love; smile and show others you recognize their worth. Treat everyone with respect whether you mind tells you they deserve it or not. Be patient as others travel the mine fields of faith while always reminding them God is standing by with road signs to enable them to complete the journey. Do not judge and condemn decisions; just let them know God is there to help when they are ready. Recognize that in a hectic world filled with responsibilities there is still time to care about others. And still time to pray for them. And always time to teach others about God by being constantly aware that your actions can encourage or destroy. Choose wisely, my friend.

P	**Praise God**
L	**Love God**
A	**Acknowledge the Blessings and Anticipate His Presence**

Those who believe in God and accept Jesus as Savior and realize that a great deal of our wise counsel comes from the Holy Spirit are a blessed people. Too often we may ignore the source of our blessings, and pride takes the credit. We are human beings who still make mistakes. One of the greatest mistakes is not recognizing God's protection and love that often arrives in the form of a blessing. In so many, many circumstances the good you encounter and enjoy is not of your doing. You did not create it; you received it. Yes, you may have played a part. No doubt you tried to do that anyway. But even success that occurs because of your actions frequently contains a surprise that you did not and could not create. You may not have even known you needed it to be created!

The knowledge of 'how' something occurred does not replace the knowledge of 'why.' The 'why' is because God is love. He wants us to know something we did not; He wants us to experience or understand something we could not. He wants to protect, to guide, to remind us of the love He has for us. He sees our needs and welcomes our efforts to achieve, but He also wants to be involved in our daily lives, to work alongside us, to share in the joys of knowing something wonderful has been accomplished and/or given. And it is only fair to acknowledge His presence throughout by expressing gratitude.

> **The knowledge of "how" something occurred does not replace the knowledge of "why."**

Trust God in the small 'things' as well as the large ones. It is in our nature to demand understanding, but sometimes God's plan is beyond our limited understanding. Sometimes the reasons 'why' might frighten or even seem undesirable. But the 'Why of God' is always just perfect, regardless of whether it is obvious at the time or not. Just trust the One who never changes. Trust He does not have cranky or mean days; everything He does is done in love. Let me include the fact that frequently those 'bad days' are the product of our own actions. Yet, God is always there to use consequences of our sin to create something wonderful, if we let Him. Key to success? Look for Him in the midst of…well, in the midst of life. Good is happening! May I say, "God is Happening!"

Life does not always turn out the way we planned. Dreams, hopes, preparation for the future while we are young may lose a little of their sparkle as we grow older and mature. If you look closely, though, you can see that each and every event in your life has brought you to today, prepared you for this moment – through hardship and hurt, through rebellion, through foolish thoughts and actions, through sadness and through joy and knowledge provided by the Bible. The fact you made it this far is undeniable proof that God has been with you through it all. He was present; He is present; He will be present always.

Our problem, however, is that often we forget to look for His presence. If we did the difficulties might not seem so tragic. The roadblocks would be only temporary to allow construction for your future. Do not fear; pray and trust.

Our greatest blessings can be in the moments we see God's arrival in daily life. Wisdom from your brain that you did not anticipate. A calm spirit in the midst of chaos. Joy instead of fear. Love in the midst of the world's hate. Those are all gifts given daily and just waiting for eyes to be opened and hearts to realize the God is nearby. He is always nearby, but time pressures and conflict can often close our eyes to His presence. Begin today to spend each moment anticipating God's presence throughout your day. The moment you recognize the wonder of that much power, love and protection you will begin to see the world and your life in a different perspective. I promise.

P	**Praise God**
L	**Love God**
A	**Acknowledge His Blessings and Anticipate His Presence**
N	**Negotiate Nothing when it comes to God's Will for your Life.**

Negotiate Nothing may seem an unusual wording for your plan. Perhaps you could substitute compromising your faith in God or your belief in His plan for your life, ignoring your needed gratitude for Jesus' sacrifice on the cross at a time you need something from God and don't have the willingness or 'time' to acknowledge the magnitude of the sacrifice in that moment. Yet, 'negotiation' seems better suited. Remember stories of the soldier's prayer in the foxhole under fire? God, if you let me live, I will do anything you ask of me. Bargaining at its best and a most urgent example of negotiation. Immediate need, the desire to survive, no promise is too extravagant if God will only let one endure, live through, survive the moment. Merriam Webster defines Negotiate as "to discuss something formally in order to make an agreement; to get over, through, or around (something) successfully." Close your eyes and picture yourself in a chair trying to convince God that life is simply too hard, and it might be better if He would only take away the problem or eliminate the cause of the problem. In exchange you will…

Do you remember the character from the Popeye cartoon who did a little negotiating of his own?

Offering to pay another day if he could only have a hamburger today. Somehow, I believe many of my generation could quote his words exactly. That character was relentless;

always offering the same negotiation, never changing his desires, yet always acknowledging his pledge to repay at a later date - always going to the only one who could provide that hamburger. I have tried and tried to remember an episode in which he did actually pay his debts on a Tuesday and can't remember one. Yet his heart must have seemed to be in the right place because his "credit" was always good enough to get the hamburgers.

When we decide to negotiate with God it is pretty safe to say we feel our heart is also in the right place. At least in that moment. Truly, consider the many times way leads on to way, and we forget the promises we made after the hurt, need, or desire has been dealt with? Have you ever discussed a change in path with God – trying to tell Him you know a better way or would at least work just as hard succeeding somewhere else. Your negotiation includes future gratitude for a different opportunity, a desire for Him to understand your insecurities, an explanation for why your life does not seem to have time right now. Years later you awake to find life was only presenting a distraction to take you away from God's path and idea of success. Thomas Edison said, "A good intention, with a bad approach often leads to a poor result." Laurence Boldt clarifies, "Good intentions are not enough; commitment and sacrifice are necessary." Laying truth on the line Norman Vincent Peale states, "Good intentions are no substitute for obedience."

That is the bottom line…God has presented instruction throughout your Bible. The Ten Commandments in Exodus 20 were designed to guide and protect you – but how often are they ignored because many feel resentment that God would dare think He has the right to govern one's life? The

Great Commission in Matthew 28:19-20 reminds you of your God-given purpose and presented with instruction for sharing your faith; the parables of Jesus contain so much wisdom for those willing to look for the parallels to life as you know it. Failure to listen to instruction leads to: discipline in school, discipline after playing ball next to a new lamp in the living room, discipline after beating up your little brother, or discipline for not taking out the trash. All examples bring consequences and discipline. And we usually live with the thought of consequences before and after the event. We accept the discipline then, and yet when some deliberately disobey God's instruction they resent His discipline with every fiber of their being. Some either characterize God as a tyrant or begin new negotiations to minimize, maybe even eliminate the discipline.

If you choose to negotiate with God about any of His commands, can you absolutely guarantee you will follow through with your promises? Absolutely guarantee your future actions? Most importantly can you guarantee that your alternative choices will still accomplish God's Will in your life and the lives of others? Will someone else suffer the consequences? And is that someone God? You? Those you love? Those who have no other way of learning about God and Jesus but through you?

Regret becomes harder to live with the older one gets, in my experience anyway. Then I remember the grace of God, the determination of God. I remember His undying desire to bring purpose and a willing spirit to His children. Those with good intentions never give up! Isn't that a great description of God as well? Second chances, grace, mercy, guidance, love, never giving up on those He loves... My regrets remain but become tempered as I look back to see how God still provided many of the same opportunities as I grew in my faith, as I matured in my trust, and as I recognized the importance of the endeavors He was trying to bless me with. The point I really want to make here – God is never far away. He does not change, and His Plans will be realized. The choice to be involved and feel the blessing is ours to make.

On this day in God's Auction House, as you stand looking at the treasures before you and knowing the auction has begun, and decisions are waiting to be made, what will you do?

Will you allow yourself to be loved and blessed, or will you begin your own negotiation with God? The Plan provides wisdom, allows you to anticipate the joy as well as keeping you focused on the true goal.

**That Plan will continue to guide
you as the bidding ensues...
throughout your life filled with God's blessings.**

P	**Praise God**
L	**Love God**
A	**Acknowledge His Blessings and Anticipate His Presence**
N	**Negotiate Nothing when it comes to God's Will for your Life.**

**Now, add the word: 'Unconditionally'
to all parts of the Plan.**

6

---∞∞∞---

Let God Be God. You just be grateful.

"The Lord is my portion;
I promise to keep Your Words.
I entreat Your favor with all my heart.
Be gracious to me according to Your Promise."
Psalm 119:57-60. ESV

Take a moment to consider the words of that verse…it begins with the Lord; it establishes His provision and does so in the present tense "is." Not was or will be - He is. God is God, it is to our disadvantage to deny it. To acknowledge God has so many great and wonderful attributes is only the beginning though.

Note how quickly the attention turns to the speaker's need to make his awareness of God evident. "I promise." That "I" denotes a choice, that despite everything that seeks to deter one from God's path, that commitment has been made and will continue to be a guiding principle for life.

At this point it is only realistic to acknowledge that old saying, "Promises are made to be broken." Recognize right now that is not truth; that is manipulation by one who seeks to destroy.

However, admitting that keeping our promises to God is sometimes difficult, pay attention to the psalmist's quick request for God's favor. A quick read may have some believing God's favor is anything mankind could ever want. A slower, insightful read should have you considering what God's favor looks like and understand the true meaning of gratitude for one so wise.

> It is forgiveness despite our failures.
> It is strength to live each day as He guides and protects.
> It is a love that words cannot describe, but hearts can feel every moment of every day.
> It is Mercy and Grace in all endeavors, including those promises to God that we desire to keep but tend to struggle with keeping.

Thus, "be gracious according to Your Promise." Note the focus is still on God – who He is. It also shows an awareness and acceptance of known attributes of God. It shows knowledge gained through study and prayer. It is essentially an appreciation for all the psalmist has learned, accepted and desired from God. God is all in all; the psalmist trusts that. Therefore, he admits the need for further instruction from God. We all need to be reminded of that from time to time.

As you stand in God's Auction House,
in a room filled with treasures
our human minds may lack the ability to comprehend,
you may feel the need to whisper a simple prayer.
If so, please do so.

God has blessed you mightily, and the time may have come to say, "Thank You, Lord." He has made this day possible. Thank Him for the time you have been allowed to spend with Him. Thank Him for the wisdom and care He has provided in your "room" of life-giving treasure.

Thank Him for the love, mercy and
grace He has given each and
every day of your life to this point,
and so obviously desires to show in your future…

SECTION TWO

7

———⟡⟡———

This is the Day which the Lord Hath Made...

*"Oh Sing to the Lord a **new** song;*
sing to the Lord all the earth!"
Psalm 96:1 ESV

Today I found my Bible already opened to Psalm 96, and in the margin of the *Quest Study Bible* was a question for thought: "What's wrong with the old songs?" They are often more familiar but does familiar necessarily mean better? They may or may not be enough for today's challenges. Those same words we recite without thinking, the same routines we live without really living, the same struggles we seem to repeat - are they enough? Psalm 96:1 looks for a "new song," one with developing maturity, gratitude for the mercy, greater understanding and certainly a new song with clarity that today's auction is not only exciting, but it will require wisdom in our choices, self-control in our attitudes, and our trust and gratitude for each and every gift, regardless. It is important to keep our praises fresh, timely, and current. Then and only then, will daily life become manageable, and only then will we understand it is because of God.

Existence is part of the past. Life is lived in the present.

Life is given to us today to do with as we choose. Choose to praise God first and last. Recognize and be grateful God will never turn His back on us, or don't. Take the credit for the moments we survive or recognize Who held our hand through difficulty. Never consider any past praise complete without need for additional gratitude, recognition of His mercy, and power, and love and understanding, and grace, and encouragement, and forgiveness and wisdom…how many more could you add to that list if you only took a moment right now to consider who God is and all He has done? Singing a new song to the Lord is just that – recognizing each new and generous gift He provides on a daily basis. That understanding and recognition should lead to gratitude and praise for *who God is on a daily basis* as well.

We are not called to simply exist. The past alone is not enough to govern our lives in negative ways. It is today that has potential. It is today that presents anew God's grace and hope. Lessons learned and hardships endured must be allowed to develop an awareness in our daily lives, and then we take that awareness and pair it with all our Bible teaches. There we find understanding. In the Bible we find the wisdom to not only live in our present, but we see the grace to dream of a better future.

We have a responsibility as well as a privilege to learn

and grow from those lessons daily. We have a responsibility to look for God each and every day and allow Him to guide and teach us as we live our lives. As hard as it is to sometimes admit, we do have more to learn, more to be grateful for, and we certainly have more mercy and blessings to be recognized. Choose to never overlook that in the midst of "life." It is so very important to our todays and our tomorrows.

Lamentations 3:22-23 ESV says, "*The steadfast love of the Lord never ceases; His mercies never come to an end; they are new every morning...*" The question begging to be asked is, do we simply ignore rather than acknowledge and express gratitude for those new blessings, new mercies, new gifts every morning? *One*, you woke up – even on a bad day that one fact truly is hope illustrated. *Two*, there will always be someone to greet you with love and hope for the day. He is God. *Three*, it is a privilege to spend time with the One who provided those gifts.

Four, just choose to do it!

Start each day with God; Live in your present and commit to live in your future experiencing God's love, forgiveness, mercy, excitement and teaching in both present and future.

Charles Dederich said, "Today is the very first day of the rest of your entire life." That simple statement conveys so much more than many ever stop to realize. By God's grace you are here. You are still loved. God has granted you mercy that will allow you to begin again if needed. Jesus made that possible by His death on the Cross to guarantee that evil can never overtake or destroy you. You have the chance to be grateful for opportunities coming your way - yesterday's mistakes cannot limit your potential today unless you let them. Do you truly recognize the hope in those words? Those mercies that make life not only possible but glorious! Do you choose to recognize God who stands nearby to ensure that hope and mercy? It is entirely up to you, but I so hope, for your sake, that you will choose to make that commitment today. I promise you won't regret it. Even if…

Today, you are tired. Bills need to be paid; work has to be done, and life has to be lived. We all have responsibilities, and life can quickly encourage us to forget that our first responsibility is to God - if we let it. In the midst of daily stress God is often relegated to the "Land of Later." Forgotten is the mercy; remaining are the wishes for the big blessings that could make life easier…Money trees in the backyard, Energy and good health to accompany us on an adventure rather than a day of responsibility. We seek unconditional love from bosses, family, folks on the freeway, and ourselves as well. Life is forever changing and evolving into the life we are choosing.

And God is ever waiting, providing that unconditional love, simply waiting for us to involve Him in our daily lives.

Honestly ask yourself:

Are your actions choosing a life without
God - maybe not consciously or entirely,
but are you withholding the invitations that welcome Him
into every aspect of your life and not just a chosen few?

Are you ignoring the opportunities to hear His Voice
and see His presence throughout days of responsibility?

Are you suffering and longing for more to
life without taking necessary steps
to provide the joyous foundation of mercy
and love God offers each morning?

Are you willing to forget yesterday's
trials and tribulations, and
begin each day praising God and thanking
Him for what is to come?

No more "same song, second verse" but rather: New Mercies, New Perspective, New Joy,

New Recognition of God before taking on the world. And New Praise for Him.

Choose a willingness to build a new and improved, stronger foundation in God.

Allow yourself to become open to a new awareness of just how deep the love of Jesus is.

Be ready to be amazed anyone could love you so very, very much!

Isn't that a great way to begin a day of responsibility? And, truthfully, isn't it a good way to close out the old ones?

8

---∽∽---

Know God and then, you can Truly Know Yourself...

"Train up a child I the way he should go..." Proverbs 22:6 KJV

We all have that inner child living within us – the one who loves (whether we admit it to others or not) playgrounds, birthday cake, cartoons, kicking a ball across the yard, caramel apples and so much more. They bring back memories of childhood, or they can create new memories in place of a childhood lost or an innocence lost.

It is safe to say we all want joy, happiness, and safety. If it is not the first thing we see as we endeavor to live an adult life of purpose, or worth, or peace we find ourselves trying to create it. One way or another.

Run through this list to see how many exemplify your desires:

The colors of Disney - the primary colors that shine so brightly and seem uncomplicated like the Mickey Mouse "Hot Dog Dance." No skill required, just fun. And the older we get the more we desire just a little fun to overcome the responsibility, the stress, and the confusion that asks, "How did I get here?"

The beautiful child you are raising – the one whose life allows you to be a child again as well, to express your childlike excitement over a baby animal or to utilize your trip to an amusement park to shop for cartoonish staplers, tape dispensers, etc. for that adult, "full of responsibility and earning dignity among your peers" desk at work. No desk at work? Answer this: just how many coffee cups fill your cabinets with humorous sayings? Do any of your cooking utensils have the shape of animals; do your favorite recipes include Rice Krispy Treats, Chocolate Chip Cookies, Macaroni and Cheese? By the way, I know adults are told to avoid the sugar and carbs, etc., but in reality, do you find yourself tempted because you just need to feel like an innocent, healthy child once in a while?

Do you ever just want to pull the covers over your head and stay in bed? To let someone else be the adult? To deny any responsibility you have in completion of a task, or the need to meet a deadline, or to even having to please others? Or worst of all, is there something you would rather not do, you don't have time for, or something that you wish was someone else's responsibility?

At this point, I will end the list…perhaps I am sharing too much of myself! Do you ever do that? Do you ever realize mid-sentence that examples of reality are beginning to sound more like your perspective and needs than the person you are trying to connect with? Empathy is a good thing, but too much of me, or you, can easily mislead others…

**UNLESS THE SOURCE OF OUR STRENGTH,
THE SOURCE OF OUR LOVE,
THE SOURCE OF OUR
KNOWLEDGE AND WISDOM
IS ONE MORE POWERFUL, MORE LOVING,
AND MUCH MORE WISE.
HIS NAME IS GOD.**

His Address is the same as yours – Understand He is, or can be, living within you, guiding, loving, teaching. He is always with you.

His office hours are eternal.

His desk is covered with items that remind Him of you and your time spent with Him. His heart breaks over your mistakes and rebounds over your confession. His love never changes. His wisdom never fails. He desires to train us UP into the people we would hope to be if we only took the time to stop and consider who God is and all that He has and will do in our lives if we only let Him. Please note the use of the word UP as in successful, wiser, happier, not DOWN as in depressed, frustrated or oppressed.

"Train up a child in the way he should go and when he is old" (and stressed and frustrated and frightened and disappointed and lost) "he will not depart from it." Proverbs 22:6 NIV. Right now, in this moment it would benefit all of us to truly accept our responsibility in training our inner child to be all that God intended and to recognize that since it truly is God's desire, He will not let us fail in the endeavor. *Perhaps you need to read that last sentence aloud – several times.*

Begin to help that inner child, to let him or her understand that your life truly does matter.

It is time to understand the love that is waiting to teach you how valuable you are to God, the love that says you are loved and protected when you decide it is time to take a leap of faith.

It is important that your inner child realizes that you are uniquely and wonderfully made for a purpose, not simply created to fill an office chair or to lead the rally for change, or as some would desire – to destroy any and all who stand in the way of selfish desires. That inner child is the one whose innocence creates a spirit of "all things are possible," Philippians 4:13a KJV, but it is also the one who can so easily get lost in the chaos. We must choose, with conviction, to teach our inner child that one must read the full sentence, hear the full thought, consider the truth in its entirety. It is time to know and accept that "all things are possible for those who love the Lord...." Philippians 4:13 KJV. Please open your Bible and read the rest of the verse. Knowledge requires time and discipline; do not place yourself among the many who fail to see that knowledge takes time to acquire. And effort.

9

"If"

*"If my people who are called by My Name
shall humble themselves, and pray,
And seek my face, and turn from their wicked
ways, then I will hear from Heaven
and will forgive their sin, and will heal their land."*
II Chronicles 7:14 KJV

Have you ever considered the impact, the power of the word "IF?" There is more power in that two-letter word than most any other word in the English language. **If** can signal wondrous, exciting results. **If** can be indicative of our anxiousness to bargain and insure we are secure with the outcome. **If** can be filled with regret or the desire for a second chance. **If** can lay the groundwork for our control over some aspect our lives. **If** can simply be an excuse for poor choices and failure. **If** can also be just the beginning of a glorious salvation that makes life worth living and insures our future in Heaven with Christ. **If** is always a choice.

IF we are willing to accept God's Wisdom and Salvation offered through His Son, Jesus...

IF we are willing to trust that the truths within our Bible were written to help the individual...

IF we are willing to live like we believe God is truly God...

IF we acknowledge that phrase, 'God is God', we really must admit that we are not.

And then, there are more applications of the word IF that are not so positive or true.

IF God is God how can I possibly be responsible for my sin? Wouldn't God destroy sin if He hated it so much? Wouldn't He take it away? Wouldn't He defeat sin to make life easier for us, eliminate the temptation so we didn't have to make so many mistakes? I know this is thin ice, but consider how often mankind looks for others to blame for our failures. And if no one is around then how often do people say, "God, how could you allow this is to happen? You brought that person into my life. I didn't go there planning to sin; You presented the temptation, right?"

The bottom line here is that important word: CHOICE. And those choices often begin with "If." The problem is that far too frequently "If" signals another bargain.

> IF I allow God to count me among His People does that mean I have to put forth effort even when I don't have the time or energy or motivation? Doesn't God understand that my line of work has no time for humility, so it really is not my strongest personality type.

Could that "called by My name" simply be a text that I can reply "Not Now" or "Will contact you later" or "I am driving right now" so please do not interrupt.

IF I trust God I will expect big things in return. God, don't tell me what You want;

I have needs too, you know.

IF I share my faith or witness in any form, I want to see life-changing results in those I have focused on (and far too often that "in others" include those we wish to change.) And by the way, I know you are God, but if you will just trust me I know what needs to be changed. And, I would prefer to see the results immediately and not just be content to know I planted a seed others will see come to fruition."

Reader, I know some of these things sound a little shocking, but the reality of our words and actions is often harsher than we are willing to admit. We lack the wisdom and the authority to ever tell God what to do, but in the seconds before we remind ourselves of that fact have you ever wanted to say things just like that? God wants honesty from His children; on the other hand, honesty is not always pretty, nor does it always lie within spiritual nicety guidelines. Rather than deny what we want to say, instead letting it fester within our spirits while we say the right words in our prayers, is not honesty. (Side note: honesty does not equal disrespect. Period.)

Isn't it just more honest to share what we are feeling and release all the negativity and sometimes all the nonsense we are thinking so that it is released, leaving our minds and sometimes our bodies open to be filled with God's ideas and wisdom and leadership? There is room for honesty with God, but we must all recognize one important caution: the only danger in leaving a *gripe session* without allowing God to speak is the quickest way to fail in just about everything. Listening to God is paramount, and regardless of time constraint or attitude or pressure of any kind, our place is to sit quietly and let God speak – until He is through speaking. He graciously listens to us. We must offer Him the same courtesy. Period.

Our privilege is that we will then be wiser and ready to praise God for His love. Our Greatest Blessing is to experience God, see Jesus, and feel the counsel of the Holy Spirit as God teaches us great and mighty things we really, really need to know.

But, only if we are willing to be completely honest in an effort to become completely in-tune with the One who loves us completely. Anything that stands between your relationship with God, anything at all, that creates roadblocks to your faith, to your understanding, to your soul must be acknowledged.

Years ago, when I was struggling to recover my foundation, that which had previously made me feel like God was proud of me, I returned to my home church. That was where wonderful teachers and my pastor had talked to me directly about God's plans for His children. That was where God's commandments were taught with respect and the need for obedience. That was where my mother had taken me every Sunday to ensure I never missed a single lesson from the Bible. However, as a young adult I made some poor decisions while on my own in college. I knew they were leading me to a path that God had never told me to follow. I knew that, but I chose to seize the wrong opportunity anyway. First mistake: I had not made the effort to find a church that kept me grounded in my responsibility to God and surrounded me with wise counsel. Second mistake: I made poor choices despite that little voice in my mind offering a better way. I suffered then and was left with the consequences for many years.

Eventually, I moved back to my home church and was reminded of who I was meant to be, despite my imperfections. I again surrounded myself with growing Christians who encouraged and loved me as I navigated the mine field of consequences of my actions. And my joy was complete – or almost. I still felt guilty about poor choices and could see that others had to suffer the repercussions of my actions as well. That broke my heart, but I could not say it aloud even to God for fear He might realize I deserved more consequences. I laugh now; are you laughing at me or with me? And then entered Jim.

He was my Sunday School teacher. Wise, kind, biblically grounded, and his teaching always had my full attention. And then… one Sunday he talked about honesty in prayer. His illustration stunned me, "Sometimes you just have to stomp your foot and yell out 'God, life is not fair!'" His tone and additional words had a shock value that day. No one else in my church had ever sounded that angry with

God – in my opinion, it bordered on disrespect for One who deserved nothing less than full respect. I *literally* fell out of my chair and was convinced my childhood pastor rolled over in his grave…Jim simply and graciously waited for me to regain my seat and continued. "If you cannot be totally honest with God you can never have the relationship you want and need to survive in this world." Yes, Jim's attitude would have carried severe punishment in my home as well as my school. But, on that day I learned I could tell God the truth of my struggles, thus creating room for God's answers to the problems consuming my life. I admitted that all the rehearsed prayers and words describing a gratitude that I did not always feel, including words conveying a faith in my future that I did not always have, did not allow me to always approach God's throne of grace in complete honesty. To be less than honest is still a lie. But, keep in mind, honesty must still always be given with respect – especially when being honest with God.

I was given a chance to expel the negative emotions and then ask God to replace the negatives with His – well, with His everything! It is a lesson I carry with me to my present. John 3:30 NIV says "He must become greater; I must become less." The wording of my prayers became a conversation between my imperfection and His desire to share His grace, love and wisdom. No longer (well, not as often) was my life made up of intense emotion that hindered our relationship; it was replaced with focus, excitement and confidence in what God was then able to teach me.

The full impact of Jim's message guides me even today. He did what was necessary to ensure my full attention. For the first time, I fully understood that entering that church building was good but insufficient to fully return me to the heart of God, that heart I had been dancing around in my prayers but never choosing to be honest enough to sacrifice the shame I was feeling inside. And while I had tried to endure the consequences of poor choices, I had left God out of the process due to a lack of total honesty. I was doing my best to substitute actions and church attendance for confession and forgiveness. I was not admitting my responsibility and my sorrow at disappointing God. I was not being fully honest.

Honesty with God is paramount if we ever hope to allow Him to be honest with us.

While it is not necessary to yell at God, it is necessary to share your emotions – you know the ones that consume your every thought? If anything consumes your every thought how will there ever be room for God and His thoughts? Open and honest conversation with God is critical. Open and honest conversation *from God* is *essential* to our ability to live a life of purpose, a life of joy, and a life as it was intended.

Granted, the idea of God being fully honest about our failures and sin seems terrifying. It is not. God's honesty always carries a measure of love and forgiveness we can only marvel at. He admits a sense of disappointment, but it often includes that second chance that enables us to use the experience or lesson learned to create an alternative path that can and will allow us to still see His love, His plan for our lives, and His joy in the fact we have chosen to return regardless of any and all mistakes, simply because we love Him.

Take a minute to again read II Chronicles 7:14 printed at the beginning of this chapter. I tend to hear that verse quoted more frequently as we are encouraged to pray for our country, our leaders and the direction of our country. However, this time I want you to read it in the context of who you are, 'the land' you have been given by God – your home, your church, your family, your blessings, and the opportunities you are given each and every day. Acknowledge that homes often need healing after anger, hurt or discouragement. Understand that families and close associates often need healing simply because of words spoken without thought. Those closest to you should be considered your blessings, but even in the face of goodness there can still be competition or rebellion or a lack of the love desired. Remember how God led Joshua and the Israelites to the Promised land, but recognize they still faced opposition from opposing armies. Then, call to mind just how many times God fought the battles for them – but only after they acknowledged Him, and after they listened to His plans.

It is up to us to remain long enough in God's presence to allow Him to share ALL of His plans and love with us. Far too often we feel there is only time to say, "Hi," or ask forgiveness, or to make our requests. We talk, but we do not stay to listen.

I can promise God's voice is what you desire, even if you have never realized that. Once you allow yourself to hear His voice you will understand. There is nothing like it, nothing as wonderful and exciting, nothing that warms your soul like the voice of God.

10

And... Cue the "If Only's"

No Stage Direction Needed

*What is it in humanity that confuses
the unlimited goodness of God
with our desires to customize our acceptance of His goodness?
Why must insecurity, fatigue, doubt creep into the joy,
the praise, the wonder of God?*

People want to be successful, and the level of that desire is entirely dependent on the areas each individual has chosen as worthy of their time and effort. When the possibility of recognition of either their success or their failure enters the picture however, they may quickly revise their list of worthy goals. Accountability has entered its ugly head. It is so much easier to reach success within our own minds with no accountability because we can change the original goal to match the output. And no one knows the difference...as long as we are satisfied, right?

On the other hand, when specific guidelines are

required, and accountability cannot be denied it is up to us to rise to that challenge. We may need to admit we are not qualified to accomplish the task on our own and ask for help. We may suffer setbacks or missteps, but even those can be overcome by learning from our mistakes and trying again. We may even doubt our abilities, but then we simply need to have a little faith and return to the manual and the Teacher who encouraged all progress up to that point.

That last paragraph is a perfect illustration of God's leading and teaching in our daily lives if we will only acknowledge that He truly is the best Teacher, with the best textbook that could ever be provided, to aid us in our quest to sometimes attempt the impossible. **Faith** says, "I can't, but God can." **Determination** says, "I think I can, but I know God can." **Reality** says, "This could easily be impossible." However, Reality has no choice but to continue that thought by reading Matthew 19:26 NIV, "with God all things are possible." Without that faith, determination and the reality of God we can quickly come up with excuses not to even try.

IF ONLY …

> …I knew more
> …I had help
> …Opportunity had, or will, present itself
> …If only I had…
> …If only I hadn't…

Those 'IF only' statements tend to be based on circumstances, opportunities, knowledge, cooperation from others or the expectation that God is supposed to be the One who makes all things possible – therefore, our responsibility is quickly dismissed. Such an attitude becomes an open invitation for excuses that hope to create a polite response to any request for our time, energy or willingness to succeed at anything other than what we have chosen.

But what if we changed that wording just a little? Change "IF ONLY" to "IF I" Chose to Take a Chance on God."

"If I" focuses on self, you and me and our part in any relationship, especially our relationship with God. "IF I" focuses on our choices, our regrets, our willingness, and sometimes our failure to take a chance on God.

"IF I" truly want a relationship with God it is time for me to meet Him, to acknowledge His presence for good in my life, and understand that all worthy goals take time. Goals take work, but the rewards of a relationship with God is beyond all that is exciting and good and worth the time and effort. However, that relationship is up to the individual. God is always present, but He is never one to force His way into our lives. He presents the invitation; the RSVP is up to us.

"IF I" think of all the goodness I want to see in the world, He has already provided for it. "IF I" feel I want to make a difference in the lives of others, in society, in the world's understanding of the word "love," He has already provided the avenue leading to it. "IF I" want to trust that mistakes on my part will not doom me to a life of utter defeat for eternity I simply have to be honest in my relationship with God and admit that I have sinned and accept the forgiveness

Jesus already provided, long before I even knew I needed it. "IF I" want beauty and happiness I need merely to open my eyes to see God's Creation in all its many forms and allow myself to not only feel gratitude but to feel happiness at the way God provides for all my needs.

"IF I" want to be loved I simply have to open my heart to feel and my mind to understand that it is God alone who truly feels utter and complete love for me just as I am. And that 'just as I am' is an incredible confidence booster!

> *The Bible tells me "I am uniquely and*
> *wonderfully made..." Psalm 139:11 NIV.*
> *It is not an "If and Then" statement –*
> *it is straightforward fact.*

Now, "IF I" really want to experience that goodness, trust, beauty and happiness, that forgiveness and the "love that surpasses all understanding" in Ephesians 3:19 KJV, then the time is now to take a chance on God. And, just as taking a chance on anything truly desirable, you may experience just a touch of fear (normal), be forced to fight the battle of letting go of what we know of the world in a desire to find true treasure in God (normal). True treasure – not the glittery fool's gold that fades over time but the true 24K gold that endures throughout a lifetime. Please know God will never fail; He will never desert you; He loves you. Take a chance; Choose not to fear; Marvel at the life that awaits you; say Thank You. God chose to love you; He chose you as His beloved child; and He chooses to never leave you.

It is time to consider the following:

IF only I could... just relax, let go, and let God work I might just be amazed.

IF only I could... pay better attention to lessons learned, both the ones I enjoyed and the ones I truly did not enjoy as much, I might begin to understand God a little better.

The "IF only I could" allows one to begin to focus on an honest picture of self, good and bad choices, on regrets, on willingness and sometimes our failure to take a chance on God.

Take a moment to consider your "IF only" thoughts. Have you missed opportunities because of fear of failure or apathy or laziness or because someone else convinced you not to even try to do great and mighty things for God? Did someone else tell you it wasn't a good idea, or you were too inexperienced, or that smarter people than you had tried and failed. The one I hear frequently is "Maybe in the future; this just is not a good time." Honestly, "If not now, when?" "If not you, who?"

Tell me, as you considered the "If only" category did you find yourself thinking "If I had just" statements as well?

If I had just...

How does it go? 'Regrets... can we please just move on?'

Human beings make foolish mistakes, experience a lack of focus, find themselves in the midst of emotional reactions versus logic; and then there is doubt versus faith. It is not necessary or important to catalogue past mistakes, carry those burdens on our shoulders for a lifetime, and certainly not allow those mistakes to destroy our future in Christ. Our confession and His forgiveness ensure that regrets do not have to control our lives.

Yes, there are consequences to sin, and those are valuable lessons not to be ignored. I believe that I serve a Risen Savior who saw me coming and figured He ought to stay nearby just in case – and He did so throughout my life. There is no doubt that mistakes could have been bigger and so could the blessings. What did I miss out on? Do I take credit for wise choices? Not at all. Do I realize there were days I did my best to cause others to question my convictions? Yes, and for those I am deeply sorry. But at the end of the day, I never lost sight of my choice to choose Jesus as my Savior. I never grew so hardened of heart that I no longer realized when I chose my own path and totally ignored His. That is my greatest blessing – Jesus stuck by me through thick and thin. He made sure on the Cross that I had the opportunity to be forgiven If I only recognized the need to confess my sin. God made sure I remembered I was always loved beyond measure, regardless. And that was so important.

Daily, God makes sure I remember I am always loved, and loved completely, regardless. And that has made all the difference.

If anyone ever tries to convince you that He has given up on you or on someone you love I need you to know that is not, and never will be true. God never gives up, even in the times that it would be a justified response to our attitudes or actions. That is the best definition of divine love.

Before reading the rest of the page, take a minute to

consider your life. Any regrets? Any unconfessed sin? Any simple, "I am sorry, Lord" or "I just wanted to be sure I said "Thank You" enough. Maybe now is the time. Ecclesiastes 3:1NIV says, "There is a time for everything under the sun…" maybe this is your time to simply connect with God and say the things that life often prevents being said. Take a minute; maybe make a list; maybe just get on your knees and pray. Regardless, I can promise you it will be the best moments of your day.

Relax, let go and let God work…

This bears repeating. A good goal for tomorrow, and the next day, and…

Think things through rather than react or rely on emotional insecurities…

> This one bears repeating as well; perhaps it
> will serve as a reminder when we
> find ourselves "feeling" our way rather than
> "knowing" God's way.

Pray and obey when making choices. Did you fully comprehend that full statement? Praying is always step one. Obeying, well, let's just say, obeying tends to get lost somewhere in the long list we call life. Seriously, do we often forget how to count? 1. Praying 2. Obeying.

It shouldn't be that hard. We shouldn't make things so complicated. But we often do. Time to own up to that fact and return to that childlike innocence seen in a toddler learning to count 1, 2, 3. You are given only two and are capable of many more. However, you and I both must master that 1,2 routine first!

Acknowledge God's goodness more, God's plan earlier – and *follow through.*

Worthy goal. Do you realize that we have the opportunity to learn as much from our successes as from our mistakes? Too often we hurt more when we fail, and when the time comes to honestly analyze our part in that failure, we can begin to see the lessons provided in that failure. However, can you imagine avoiding the hurt and experiencing instead the comfort, the exhilaration present in success that only happens with God by your side? Both teaching experiences are valuable. And both are a choice. Choose wisely.

Revise your own goals; avoid failure, choose God's grace, and recognize that this is a wonderful example of God being God. Keep in mind it should never be an excuse for choosing failures, mistakes, or foolishness but rather create in us a desire to work, to choose to succeed, to create your solid foundation of a life well lived. Let that type of grace immediately lead you to humility and gratitude that God did not give up on us at times of disobedience and panic and confusion and frustration and insecurity. Through it all, God was loving and teaching, and greatest of all – God was giving us a second chance. Another second chance, and another, and another…

I don't believe it is necessary to catalogue past mistakes, carry those burdens on our shoulders for a lifetime, or to allow any mistakes to destroy our future in Christ. That statement bears repeating, repeatedly. Regrets and self-incrimination can force our focus away from the needed relationship with Jesus. Manipulation on the part of evil can convince us that we are unworthy. Yes, there are consequences to sin, and those are valuable lessons not to be ignored, but your focus must remain on the One who is willing to forgive sin if you confess it. That is my greatest blessing – Jesus stuck by me through thick and thin. He made sure on the Cross that I had the opportunity to be forgiven IF I only recognized the need to confess my sin. God made sure I remembered I was always loved beyond measure, regardless. And that was so important.

Recently, however, I have reached a point in life that I am being reminded of things I never actually (or in complete sincerity) acknowledged. Is that age, or is it God preparing me for yet another adventure? Who knows? Either way it has been eye-opening.

Truly consider for a moment just how you came to be here, in this moment, at this point in life, with your blessings and hardships, with yet another opportunity to involve God more thoroughly in your life. Consider fully the following...

> We obey; God is allowed to work.
> We disobey; God teaches through the hardships.
> We learn; we can teach.
> We fail; we see our true need for humility and God's true glory.
> We cannot undo our past, but we can restart our future!

Through it all, past, present and future God has been, and always will be merciful. Keep in mind that is not a "get out of jail free" card. Instead, that mercy is the motivating factor.

Through it all, God is present, and you will be blessed in one way or another, in God's perfect way, whether it be the one we had in mind or not. We will be blessed. **We are blessed.**

God is not dead. He is alive. And so am I; so are you – so time to get started! Pray and Obey.

And God will be glorified. Oh, and by the way, we will truly enjoy the journey!

11

"Abide in Me as I Abide in You"

John 15:4 NRS
A Promise for Eternity

"If God is for us, who can ever be against us?"
John 8:31 NLT

Accept where you are right now. We begin with an imperative statement designed to make us see that reality must be acknowledged and understood and worked through before any needed changes can be made. Mankind is quick to speak what we think we want, what we need and how to get the results we desire. However, how much of our time is devoted to today, right now rather than focusing on God and His plans for our *future*? It is up to us to see the reality of what is being taught in our Bible as we study it today. We would be wise to pay attention to what is being given by God to encourage us throughout our days right now.

Growing more and more aware of our need for God and His enabling power *today* is the platform upon which we begin preparing for our tomorrows. This time in your life should be dedicated to growth. Know who you are, accept who you can be, and begin moving forward. Today you will be given gifts of knowledge, experiences that confirm what your Bible is saying, and grace that promises your journey throughout life will not be lonely. God will always be there if you let Him. I firmly believe God is alive and well and always nearby.

Recently I saw an ad for an App called "NewsBreak" by Particle Media. While I know nothing about that particular source, nor anything about its political persuasion, its biases or lack or bias, or its authenticity, I was impressed by its slogan, "live safer, more vibrant, more truly..."

And it gave me pause. Live more truly what? Live more truly the truth; live more truly knowledgeable; live more truly passionate about your beliefs? Or could it be live more truly confident that what you hear is true; live more truly devoted to gaining full understanding; live more truly aware of all that is happening around you?

I cannot answer those questions about that particular App despite my sometimes naïve and trusting personality hoping truth is what they provide, but I also instantly realized how important that slogan is to our individual lives - How all the questions of life can be answered in an ancient source so very relevant today, the Bible. Isn't that what God infused into every aspect of our Bible? Truth.

Live safely – scripture provides wisdom and caution for everyday life and is our "truth meter" by which all information must be measured.

Live more vibrantly – You are unique. A masterpiece created by God!
"You are "fearfully and wonderfully made" according to Psalm 139:14 ESV.
Celebrate that – with confidence!
Live it with excitement! With joy. And certainly, with God.
Live life on Purpose and for a Purpose.

Live more truly – based on God's Truth.

The Big Question becomes "So how do I live more truly?"

That question is where we begin with the "Appraisal Value" of each item available for your bid today. Spoiler alert! Each item is Priceless! Just like you…

Accept where you are right now. (repeated one more time for emphasis) It is reality that must be acknowledged and understood and worked through before any needed changes can be made. If things are negative on any level it is proven that we have to know an enemy before we can defeat him. How often do you give in to procrastination? Are your priorities always in order? Have you given up at any time in the last 24 hours? And the list could go on forever, but the one that seems to be our greatest compromise is sin in our lives and the failure to confess it.

Few enjoy that particular conversation, yet it is part of that "accept where and what you are right now" as well as the often-unstated extension: and if hurting, confused, dissatisfied, start looking for the source of those emotions. And do something about it. Short and simple statement, but it lacks direction, instruction, and the encouragement we often need to actually do something about it. So, what is one to do?

Recognize God's Presence in the midst of difficulty and trust that God is the only way out.

John 15:4 NRS says, "Abide in Me as I abide you..." As I so often do, I picked up a dictionary when reading my Bible. To me, the most familiar words can allow one to understand meaning in context of a larger work, but they also can encourage the reader to continue on, rather than take the time to grasp the true, deeper impact and meaning of a word. Abide is one of those words. Merriam Webster defines it as "to bear patiently; to endure without yielding; to wait; and to accept without objection." All chosen actions that probably need a little encouragement in difficult times. That is precisely why it is included in your Bible. God offers to be patient with our human failings, refuses to give *up* on us or give *in* to anything less than the best for our lives. He is ready to encourage us in difficult times and will wait for our choice to involve Him in our day-to-day lives out of respect (but with a broken heart when we do not.) Remember, there were two parts to that title, and it began with "Abide in Me." We are blessed by what God and Jesus are willing to do for us, but what are we willing to do for Them? Are we patient when God does not answer our requests immediately? Do we ignore God's presence in favor of worldly pleasures? Do we choose to delay indefinitely our communication with God over matters we fear will not please Him? Do our actions show our conviction to be His witness to those who are hurting, or do we leave it to someone else?

Abiding is not rest without a plan. Abiding in Christ is prepping for action – it is all about God: His strength, His plans, and His willingness to forgive sin if we would only confess it. And please don't miss that wonder of God's Will to provide a way to be more than we ever dreamed, more than we sometimes understand, but definitely more than mankind could ever help us to be! It is about God's Will and our willingness to obey!

We are our own worst enemy, especially in front of a plate of brownies fresh from the oven, which seems rather innocent, but we have to acknowledge that tragically there is a list of much more serious actions throughout life that can make us God's worst enemy. Recently, I have heard the following statement from a multitude of sources...

"No defeat is final unless we allow it to be."
Unless we choose defeat over hard work,
over love, over obedience, over fear or
even if we choose a lack of faith in God
and refuse an acknowledgement

**of the saving grace of Jesus over temporary
pleasure in circumstances
or dependence on earthly things, defeat
simply cannot be inevitable.**

God never fails, never gives up, never walks
away in defeat.

That is called Amazing Grace.

God works tirelessly while we often 'take
a day off.'

God never questions His identity or His
plan, or His love for us.

God continues to be God while we stumble
around trying to decide our own identity,
while we "talk the talk" but lack the conviction
to "walk the walk."

What is it in us that so often tries to choose platitudes
or excuses over action? We *work* at confusing our identity
on a daily basis. How? By our failure to accept God in all
situations, in all opportunities to pray, to learn, to act, and
to just simply be who He called us to be. Please know this is
not condemnation; it can be understanding gained if we are
willing to stop and consider life as we know it. Note: I said,
"we." We are learning together. Truth sometimes hurts, but
I need you to know that it also heals and provides us with
strength to move forward.

We all have to "be" someone as long as we are still

breathing. You and I are a distinct entity. It is up to us to decide who we will choose to be. Will your life be shaped by temporary fixes to struggles, to hurt, or to your desire to realize a personal dream? Will you actively pursue God and His plans for a life that makes a difference, a life that shares God's love by action and words? Will you choose to acknowledge all that has been given to you for a purpose greater than you or I could ever accomplish alone? There is wisdom to be found in Bible study and prayer; we need that help in becoming who we are graciously designed to be.

Far too often people don't want to hear God's plans unless they have first failed and experienced defeat. Only desperation sends some to God, and at least they are finally acknowledging His love. That is a good thing. Granted it would be better if we listened more closely before the mess, but as long as you are willing to listen rather than accept total defeat you have grown wiser and stronger and have experienced more hope than you could have ever imagined.

That is the first step, but you were created for greater things than a simple acknowledgement of God's existence.

You were created for more. You were created for friendship with God.

How can you know His plans for your life? Talk to Him. Thank Jesus who made it possible to have that loving, close, insightful relationship with God, without sin blocking your path. Talk honestly and listen with all your might. Wait on the Lord. Listen – again I give you intentional repetition; Listen to God as you pray.

Look for Him throughout your day; become aware of what is happening. You may encounter others who need prayer right that moment. So pray. God may ask you to introduce him to others through your actions and words in that moment. Perhaps He will use others to remind you of your need for God. Know that God's plans are not always obvious, but every moment we seek His presence becomes a step closer to God. We have to accept that it is not up to us to know everything. We cannot ensure that life as we know it is guaranteed to be simple and straightforward and easy. But it will be WITH God – and that is all you need, regardless of struggle or difficulty or hurt.

Look for Him as you walk – you will not be disappointed. You may even find yourself excited! Choose Him and His ways and you will never be defeated in the long run.

> *Temporary hiccups are part of being human,*
> *but "temporary" is not defined as "eternal"*
> *unless you decide it will be.*

Accept your responsibility and enjoy the "fruit" of choosing God. Take time to read and truly consider Galatians 5:22-23 and the list of "Fruits of the Spirit." Honestly, can you find anything undesirable in that list?

On the other hand, I suppose we all have the choice to ignore the fact we have been blessed in ways too many to list - even while misery seems to thrive in every moment of every day. Fail to recognize that our role is to respond to God's mercy and instruction, and life becomes harder still.

Now there is another reality check that must be acknowledged. Does being a Christian insure you will always be who God intended you to be? Hardly –

> *Human beings are prone to selfishness and*
> *to thriving in our hard-headedness.*
> *Sorry, but didn't this begin "live truly?"*
> *Sometimes truth hurts.*

We will still fight against authority on some level, because we have become spoiled. Many think of God *only* as a loving Father. We like that about Him. A vending machine who freely supplies all our needs and desires. One who provides a "Get out of Jail Free Card" as in Monopoly. Many want a father figure who loves and presents wonderful gifts and who makes us feel secure despite our wrong choices. But many often ignore the fact that…

- God is also a Teacher. He is teaching that inner child inside you, the one who wants to learn but doesn't know how.
- God is a Jealous God.
- He is a trustworthy Guide.
- And He is also a Disciplinarian. It is that aspect of God as a loving Father that mankind often wants to ignore because, honestly, human beings do not like being in trouble.
- God is Wise; He is Omniscient, knowing all things at all times – including our secret sins, our compromises, and our influence on others. Let me repeat: God is wise, but we often fail to recognize that wisdom is ours for the asking. We unknowingly,

or sometimes deliberately, choose the consequences rather than take our sins to God asking forgiveness and wisdom to move forward.

- God is Faithful and Just to forgive. I realize this next statement may seem surprising, but are we even a little bit faithful to forgive God when He chooses needed discipline for our actions or chooses a path for our lives that is not in keeping with our desires? Ouch! Until those words appeared on paper, I never consciously considered that application of our childish ways.

Human beings hold grudges not only toward others, but far too often, toward God.

Have you ever heard the following statements?

"If God truly loved me, He wouldn't have allowed...

...the death of one I loved so very much
...catastrophic illness
...my broken heart
...the loss of my job and ability to provide for my family
...this failure, or delay, or this side road
...this confusion
...oppression by evil, or even allowed evil to be in the world!
...my prayers to go unanswered
...And last but certainly not rare...
He wouldn't have allowed me to do without something, anything, I really, really wanted.

Some turn away from God after loss or unwanted discipline. They reject God's presence in their lives because He asks "too much," or life is too hard. Isn't that holding a grudge?

Sometimes it seems individuals who treasure God in a number of areas of their lives look for excuses to give up on God when trouble appears in that one area they hold most dear. They refuse to worship, have no interest in learning more about God in an effort to understand current circumstances or even to entertain God's name to be spoken in their presence until it is to be spoken in vain.

And if we move past personal complaints then can you begin to see how many blame God for all the evil in the world? Did God create evil? Or was it the result of ego on the part of one who wanted to be equal to God? Even, if it began with one can you see how quickly it was adopted by others? At that point we have to recognize the role human beings play in perpetuating that evil. How have we ignored the dangers of evil and thus let it grow? What part of me and you did nothing to stop evil and then pout when it impacted our desires? And ultimately, did we then use it as an excuse to blame God? Maybe not always, but far too frequently we not only refuse to accept responsibility for our own sin, but we also refuse to stop blaming God for the evil we allowed to take root in our lives, and in our world. Let me repeat, Human beings hold grudges not only toward others, but far too often, toward God. How can we change this? How can we change our perspective, see things more clearly, understand our importance and make the choice to become all God intended each of us to be?

Simply ask Him. Let your life be filled with redirected

focus, new hope, age-old truths of the Bible. Let your choices be made with wisdom, priorities organized in truth, and joy provided by God and accepted with gratitude. That is living truly.

"As the Father loved Me, I also have
loved you; Abide in My love.
If you keep My commandments, you will abide in My love,
just as I have kept My Father's commandments
and abide in His love."
John 15:9-10 ESV

12

"Starting Over"

If I may...I would like to share a poem I used in a Bible study several years ago. It was, and is, a favorite of all who read it. We quote it often, and laugh, and identify with it - and gain awareness of the silliness of our stubborn minds, especially when it offers the common-sense, simple solution. I am always impressed with one such as Portia Nelson who can describe life so succinctly and so very, very accurately.

"There's a Hole in My Sidewalk"

"...There is a deep hole in the sidewalk.
I fall in...
It isn't my fault...
It takes forever to find a way out."

The speaker continues to follow the same path. However, pretending the problem does not exist does not prevent a repetition of the same occurrence - thus the consequences are repeated again and again. While still in denial as to exactly who is at fault, the problem becomes a "habit" – or so we are told. **And the poem continues**:

> "…I walk down the street.
> There is a deep hole.
> I walk around it."

Learning is beginning to take place. And yet, is it a guarantee one will always be aware of circumstances and surroundings and temptations? **One final stanza:**

"I walk down a different street."

Please understand there are limitations to how many lines of even a wonderfully simple, yet eye-opening poem can be used in another's manuscript. Therefore, I encourage you to find the poem online at www.goodreads.com. Search for "A Hole in My Sidewalk," by Portia Nelson.

Then, laugh and learn. Fact: Life sometimes carries surprises. How we deal with those surprises is important. We fall in the holes, deny our responsibility in the matter, and finally climb out, only to find ourselves in the same situations making the same mistakes.

You can feel the defeat, or you can laugh at yourself for being foolish, and make corrections to prevent future mistakes. And you can accept that true wisdom takes time to develop, but that is no excuse for choosing to repeat the same mistakes over and over and over.

Please take the time to locate and read the poem. You deserve a laugh today – and you always need to gain a little wisdom…

Life is filled with potholes, as well as opportunities to

avoid them. Many potholes are poor choices; some arrive unexpectedly, others are poor habits, but God is always on duty to protect, to navigate a safer path, or to simply lend a helping hand as we climb out of the hole. It is important, however that we begin to admit we can learn how to avoid them with God at our side. At that point there is no excuse or justification for finding oneself at the bottom of the hole.

And immediately, I might as well follow it with more daily reality:

"Sometimes you win; sometimes you lose."

"Defeat is never final unless you choose to make that way."

"Pull yourself up by your bootstraps."

As I considered all the euphemisms that came to mind, I realized the true depth and importance of each of these concepts. Winning and losing are simply a necessary part of life. I can learn from defeat, choose another "street" and I can learn from the understanding that enables me to see there is another, better solution. Defeat is mine to choose – and how often do I unconsciously make that choice because it is simply easier than the hard work required to succeed in my faith? Those bootstraps on the side of your boots help pull your boots on to allow walking safely as you pursue your dreams. Grab hold and move forward.

The quickest route to inevitable frustration and depression is to believe 'Life will be easy;' 'success is always guaranteed;' 'the world recognizes your unique and special personality characteristics - and is always anxious to celebrate your presence.' Blessings abound regardless. We must accept that those statements simply are not true. They only imprison our hope.

> *If experience failure today, failure yesterday,*
> *Change your Course.*
> *It is a choice – one that must be made wisely.*

Sometimes we do need to Start Over, however, it is our choice to repeat the same mistakes or to choose a new and better path offered by God – in His mercy and love. I add that last bit to emphasize that God is always kind. Period. It is not His will that we suffer from evil. But when it is thrust upon us, we have the choice to learn from it or be defeated by it. It is not His will that we feel abandoned or lost or defeated. It is His will that we recognize His presence throughout difficult days and discouraging circumstances. It is not His Will that we feel lost without hope. It is His will that we know beyond a doubt that we truly are loved, and God will never be more than a one-word prayer away – "Help!"

Reality, as so many know it, contains self-doubt, chosen misery, a better understanding of defeat than that of joy. Fight for the energy to look for God in the midst of the chaos that seems to govern your life. He is there, waiting for you to decide whether to seek Him or run from Him.

Time for a little self-reflection

If you are struggling is it possible that your foundation of faith is flawed? Are there cracks in your foundation? What building materials have you chosen? Were they strong enough to succeed in a world that does not always understand love and forgiveness and the dangers of sin? Do you experience greed, doubt, or worldly desires overshadowing your faith in the one true God? Do the world's ideas and excuses battle your acceptance of the one who gave His life on the Cross so that you might never be defeated by sin? Is it possible that some of the problems we all face in life are not the attacks of others but the self-destructive actions of our own lives?

If so, it is up to us to create a new, better foundation. Examine your life honestly and humbly; determine where you went wrong, where you left God in pursuit of earthly pleasures, where you may have decided that you knew better than God. I realize that last one was harsh, but isn't it a daily temptation to determine your steps, your plans before you spend time in prayer and Bible study? "Time's a ticking; God can wait." I have to admit that statement is harder to accept once I see it in print. Recognizing our own flaws is difficult and often so discouraging that we choose the easy path rather than the one of honesty and hard work and determination to be the person God asked you to be. It is then we encounter the same problems, the same potholes, the same sadness.

Instead...

"Sing to the Lord a new song" as it says in Psalm 96:1 ESV. **Celebrate** a stronger conviction to place Him in a position of prominence. Sing with gusto – at the top of your lungs – so that others may know Him too!

Music has been celebrating God for centuries. Those words are beautiful and heartfelt. Can you hear the rhythms in your heart? One thing I have noticed though: singing along with karaoke machines has introduced many poor singing voices to the viewing public. We laugh and encourage the vocalists as well as cringe at a few of the notes, but we also excuse the mistakes. It is good fun. However, after a lifetime spent in church, I have never heard a unpleasant note as people sing the hymns. It is the heart of the vocalist that shines. Maybe not all notes are correct, but the beauty of the words and the faces of those singing are inspiring. And that sounds wonderful. The purpose is to praise God, and that is simply good music.

God's mercies are new every day, and they deserve to be celebrated. I was grateful for the blessings I had as a child, and I should always be grateful for blessings as an adult. Again, it comes down to my choice. We must not confine our relationship with God to the past. Live in it today, in the present, and commit to live in God's love, mercy, excitement, and teachings in the future!

Honesty requires I acknowledge that today you may be tired – bills to be paid, work to be done, and life to be lived in less than perfect circumstances. Far too many responsibilities to wear those rosy-tinted glasses today. We cannot deny that life can be hard. And the danger is that we let daily life encourage us to forget our first responsibility to God.

Don't let stress overshadow God and the joy we find in Him;
don't let responsibilities allow you to forget God's presence
in every step, every event, every tear - as well as every success.

Be grateful for small blessings. Don't let your prayer life be a constant request for the big ones. The Bible says to pray about everything. No arguments here, but consider the frequency of the following prayers:

Money trees in the backyard. (note the
plural **trees**)
Energy and good health to accompany us
on adventures rather than responsibilities.
Unconditional love from bosses, children,
folks on the freeway, and from
ourselves as well!

Life is forever evolving into the life we are choosing.

Are you choosing a life without God? Be honest with
yourself. Some may be offended at that question and respond
with a "No, I am not – I go to church; I am kind to others; I
avoid sin as best as I can with the life I am required to live!
What more do you want me to do?" I applaud your efforts,
but are you also withholding the invitation for God to feel
welcome in every aspect of your life, and not just a few?

Are you ignoring the opportunities to hear His voice
minute by minute, and do you choose not to realize that He
is present throughout your days of responsibility?

Are you suffering and longing for the joyous foundation
of mercy and love God offers each morning so that the rest of
your day is filled with hope? One of our greatest temptations
is to act because we have been taught that is measurable
progress. Thus, we dress for work, feed the family, make
the bed, and rush out the door – all measurable. What if
you decided not to "do" before you decided to "learn" more
about how to live the life you are given this day by reading
your Bible and saying/listening in a time of prayer first?

Are you choosing instead to forget yesterday's trials and

tribulations and begin each day praising God and thanking Him for what is to come?

No more "same song, second verse" filled with the same troubles of yesterday and no relief - much less joy. Life with God is filled with new mercies, new perspectives, new joy, and we should be experiencing a new recognition of God before taking on the world each new day. Are you looking and listening? Are you building that strong foundation with God each day? Are you recognizing just how deep the love of Jesus is —how deep, how consistent, how amazing it is that anyone could love you so very, very much?

What a way to begin a new day! And perhaps, what a way to close out the old ones…

13

―――❦―――

Time for a Little Conversation?

Better Yet! Time for a Little Prayer...

This may be my most difficult chapter to write. Prayer is personal and not something to be challenged, if it is genuine conversation with God. Many prayers have been taken from scripture and introduced for recitation. And they are beautiful. Reciting a written prayer is never wrong if one's heart and mind are truly focused and honest in the meaning of the words - especially, if the recipient of that prayer is God who is honestly treasured. Prayer may be emotions tumbling forth or ideas shared in excitement. It may be private or in the company of others. It may be grammatically correct. or it may be disorganized thoughts uttered in urgency. If it is intended to be genuine communication with God it is always good, and beautiful.

Prayer can become a natural desire to both honor God and to spend time talking with Him. While spending time talking to God in an honest and respectful manner is critical, know that sitting still long enough to hear Him as He speaks to you is needed as well.

I grew up in an age when the schools began each day reciting "The Pledge of Allegiance" and "The Lord's Prayer." Our allegiance to our country was to be taken seriously. Standing straight, hand over the heart, and clear enunciation of each and every syllable.

And, the words of "The Lord's Prayer" were given full honor; there was no disrespect, no fidgeting, no excuse good enough to avoid that simple prayer. It became such a part of individual lives that many from my generation can recite it without hesitation today. Those who attended church often found themselves explaining the word, Hallowed, to classmates. Some just kept asking if God's name was really Hal. There was no disrespect in the questions asked. That prayer was a subject all were interested in and sought to understand the reason it was repeated daily. The fact that school children took the time to discuss the meaning of it insured the words were not random recitation; their conversation demonstrated learning and confirmed understanding. The result was that we recognized the importance of prayer, regardless of any church affiliation, or lack thereof. The placement at the beginning of the school day demonstrated its significance. And it was accepted as a part of our routine.

The point I want to make is that allegiance to country and prayers to God were the foundation, the first idea presented in the school day. It is not that way today, and we as a people and a nation have suffered.

I taught high school for 20 years, and during that time the first idea presented in the school day was not always the Pledge and certainly was not prayer. There was a time we were to recite the Pledge of Allegiance, but it was not honored. Eventually the Pledge was relegated to Fridays. And then, it was eliminated altogether.

I miss that act of honor given in my school days. I wish students today could see the importance to their lives, and then understand the need for respect for both God and country must remain. But they need to be offered opportunities to learn first.

Occasionally, the loudspeaker might request a "moment of silence" for somber events. Those who understand the importance of prayer bow their heads, but those who have never been taught its purpose, much less who to pray to seem just plain lost. A 'moment of silence' only does not convey or teach honor in the way prayer does.

Prayer for me is best described as a personal relationship, and it continues throughout my day. A simple good morning, Lord; A cry for help in times of confusion or pain; it is a time for enjoying God's grace, His love, and His humor and saying. "I Love You, Lord." I wonder how many of us ever actually profess our love for God in our prayers. It is only recently that I find myself saying "I Love You, Lord" rather than only saying "Thank You" and not clarifying I feel so much more than gratitude.

I also enjoy His presence in my life. Did you know God has a sense of humor? I remember driving through Houston during a downpour with broken windshield wipers. Vision of the interstate was impossible, sitting on the shoulder under an overpass just did not feel as safe as I would have liked. So, I prayed, and prayed again, and prayed again. On that day God heard all the reasons I would really appreciate the rain coming to an end. He heard my fear of being hit as the rain obscured another driver's vision. He heard my promise to get those windshield wipers repaired as soon as I reached home. And, eventually - before anyone ran into my car, the rain stopped. Celebration took place in a steering-wheel-pounding expression of absolute joy! Please know that as I pounded that steering wheel I also shouted, "Thank you! Oh, You saved me! Thanks for listening! You are awesome – not just because I am safe in the rain but because I am grateful I can come to You in times of trouble." Do not consider my tone of voice to be super-religious or somber. I was shouting in excitement, in much the same tone you hear in a child when excited. My words tumbled out of my mouth. That inner child in me had a regular party as I drove the 30 miles home! But the story does not end there.

As I neared my house I fully relaxed and again expressed my relief that the rain stopped; God let me drive home safely. In my rather profuse manner, I could not stop talking…and then, a raindrop hit my windshield. Then another, then three more. And my tone changed a little. I reminded God I only had one more mile to go. I asked nicely, saying please. And then I felt something inside. There was no mistaking it. God said, "HaHa, gotcha ya!" And the raindrops stopped. Without my ever trying to analyze it, God showed His sense of humor that day, and I knew that beyond any shadow of doubt. And I laughed.

God and I have been friends a long time. I know Him, and He knows me. But it was the first time in my life that I knew I had seen and heard a joke from God. Perhaps it took gaining spiritual maturity or complete dependence on Him, taking my eyes off of myself to let God just have a little fun with a friend. And that is what He is; not a distant monarch seeking only to rule with stiff commands and stern face. He is a friend. Until He is given that place in our daily lives; until we stop to see Him, to involve Him not only in our lives but in conversation like we have with our friends on earth… Until He is allowed full access to our lives we cannot truly understand the world around us, and we miss out on the joy of that friendship.

Just one more short "share time" if I may. On that day I saw God's humor. On another day I saw the world's chaos. At a time in my life when the future was so uncertain and the present was so hard, and my entire life seemed to be crumbling, I finally chose to go directly to God. But I was ashamed to ask for His help knowing that the chaos was my fault.

One day I simply collapsed on the floor and began praying through my tears – not for removal of the chaos but for only five minutes of peace and a chance to gain strength to live the life that was spinning out of control. "Five minutes, Lord, please. Just five minutes…". And before I even realized what I was saying I saw that I was spending that five minutes *with* God.

I returned to 'my world' following those five minutes, and to be honest I found myself right back on the floor requesting just another five minutes before the day ended. And this time, I said 'thank you' and asked for just five more. This process, this request, this time in prayer went on for months, and eventually, I began to laugh as I sat on the floor, "Sorry God, it's me – Can we spend some more time together? Please." And we did. Before long I began to realize just how many blessings occurred in my life and that I no longer had to run crying to my "Five Minutes spot." Soon I could dance merrily to that same spot and enjoy the best conversations with God!

The Best! I still treasure the lessons learned and love given in my "Five Minutes spot." The joy and honesty in spending time with Him still remain a priority in my day. He knows my laundry list; and if I need to explain it I will, but for now I just enjoy being with my friend.

One lesson learned through those times and a poem given to me as a gift have served to remind me of those days throughout my life. It made a difference in my life then, and it continues to do so today. I want to share it with you – once again it is necessary to paraphrase. However, look for this poem online. However, a simple search on google or yahoo will take you to the verses immediately. Pinterest has examples of artwork containing the poem; those too might simply give your heart an extra touch of warmth as you read the 'commentary' on life as we experience it. The purpose, though, is that I want you to truly consider each line. My paraphrase is consistent with the meaning, but the life in the original verses is a gift. Please look it up.

"The Difference"

By Grace Naessens

"I got up early one morning and rushed right into the day.

I had so much to accomplish that I didn't have time to pray…"

The poem continues as one encounters problems, questions, and *then God speaks*. It mentions desires for beauty, days lacking it, and *then God speaks*. The poet begins to experience difficulty in finding God throughout the day; no effort to reconnect with Him seems to work, and *then God speaks.*

The heart of the poem is seemingly inspired by, once again, wisdom from the Bible. Didn't I tell you it has everything you need to navigate this life?

> "Ask, and it will be given to you;
> Seek, and you will find.
> Knock, and it will be opened to you.
> For everyone who asks receives, and
> the one who seeks finds,
> and to the one who knocks it will be opened."

Matthew 7:7-8 ESV

Truly, God is the only one capable of providing everything we need, whether we know how to put our hurts and desires into words, or not. We are simply encouraged to approach Him with faith in who He is and gratitude for all He has done, and a sincere desire to learn from and serve Him daily.

The poet, in only five stanzas, presented our need for God and His wise response to difficulties we seem to insist upon creating. This might be one of those "tape it to your bathroom mirror," or "frame it beautifully by your front door" moments. Give yourself the gift of acknowledgement of the grace of spending time in prayer. And now, the poet shares the profound understanding that all can benefit from in **"The Difference" continued:**

> *"...I woke up early this morning and*
> *paused before entering the day.*
> *I had so much to accomplish that I had to take time to pray."*

SECTION THREE

14

—◦◦◦—

Bidding for a Roomful
of Miracles

Though the mountains be shaken, and the hills be removed,
yet my unfailing love for you will not be shaken
nor my covenant of peace be removed,"
says the Lord, who has compassion on you."
Isaiah 54:10 NIV

Are you ready for this incredible auction to begin? Can you feel the excitement in the air? Everyone you pass in the hallway wishes you well, smiling as they remember the joy they had when it was their turn to begin the bidding. Seriously, is there really music playing as you and the Owner make your way to that special area reserved just for you?

Just a moment please - I do believe I am seeing a skip in your step. Has the joy rubbed off on you already? Yes, I do believe it has. Oh, what a wonderful day this will be! It already has been. I am definitely starting to share your excitement – and it's not even my "Lot" in life to bid on!

Now tell me, how will you ever choose the items to take home? Or do you even have to choose?

Will you bid on the entire lot and take it home now? Do you even have room for everything – that is a large room God has filled for you. Are you sure you are ready for it all at one time?

Realize that if you store your treasures, even for a short period of time, you will probably need a storage facility nearby, but will it be open when you really need your treasures? Will they become dusty or damaged while in storage? Knowing human nature, you probably won't even remember which box you placed each item in!

There is a pause…you gasp!

What will you do if the storage facility is closed at just the wrong time? Can you gain access to your treasures? What if you can't find the item you need?

Turning to avoid answers you just don't have right now, you notice the sign above the door:

Feel free to store your treasures here.
Free security provided.
Immediate access granted at all times.
Simply call 1-800-Bel-ieve.

There will be a Guide on duty to help you locate and
select the treasure most needed
at the time of your visit.

I recognize that sigh of relief. Been there, done that. Perhaps you need a few moments to consider your life and the needs of your present while still creating a platform for the desires for your future.

You smile as some passer-by rushes to share one last thought. "Don't miss the barrel by the exit door as you leave! Be sure to take an extra scoop of "love" each time you visit. Oh, don't worry – that barrel is always full...don't know how the Owner manages it, but I have never seen it empty."

And you are left alone with the Auctioneer. Today's bidding will take place in this room, your room. In an effort to experience the full "auction house atmosphere" the Auctioneer hands you a paddle with the numbers 316 written on it. His instructions are to raise that paddle when you are ready to begin and again when it is time to bid on the individual items you have chosen today. Please note: your Guide will be nearby taking notes on your selections as well as creating a list of items you are not in need of right this minute. The objective is not only to create a reminder of this incredible day but to ensure that nothing you will need for the future ever gets lost or misplaced. His job is to be sure that nothing God has created or promised for you can ever be taken from you.

The caveat here is that you realize nothing must ever take the place of God's treasures; they must not be ignored; they must not be allowed to gather dust or decay for lack of respect; they must not be manipulated or negotiated in any way. Each and every one is to be celebrated, appreciated and the Owner acknowledged as you receive "every good and perfect gift."

And now, we move to Auction Terminology...

15

.oo.

Terminology for this "Auction of a Lifetime"

Lot   *Group of objects for sale at auction*

Items selected specifically for your life,
selected by the Owner of the Auction
House in an effort to teach, protect, guide
and love you eternally.

Paddle   *Handheld device displaying the number*
assigned to an individual bidder
throughout the auction.

Paddle is to be raised for each item participant
chooses to bid on and remain raised until bid
is acknowledged by The Auctioneer.

Each participant's winning bid will be
recorded in the *Book of Life* to prevent any
future confusion.

Provenance   *Authentication Process establishing chain of ownership from date item created. Can significantly impact the value of an object.*

Chain of Ownership for each item offered has been verified and recorded as: "Each and every unique creation available is offered by God who created the world "in the beginning.""

Valuation   *Current value of property is prepared by the Auction House staff.*

Value of every item up for sale today is stated as "Priceless."
Auction House staff include: God, Jesus and the Holy Spirit

As Is   *Property for sale at auction is offered "as is," sold with all existing faults and imperfections.*

However, due to the uniqueness of this particular auction all items on display are considered "perfect." Bidders are accepted "As Is."

Cataloguing   *Factual information includes name of maker, year of its creation, and detailed description of items.*

Creator is God; Items were created before the beginning of the world in anticipation of this particular event. The distinguished and thoroughly detailed Catalogue for this particular auction is *The Bible.*

Consignor   *Owner who is transferring property to an auction house, allowing the Auctioneer to act as agent on His behalf.*

Owner of all property is God, and He has chosen to make each item available to anyone who is willing to give glory and honor to Him.

God has transferred each item to Jesus the Auctioneer who will welcome all who believe and accept His offer of forgiveness of sin, and whose names will appear on the guest list for this special event.

Designation *Consignor of a lot is sometimes identified through a designation line. The designation may identify the current owner by name or through a descriptive title.*

In this case the Designation Line will include the following:
Lord God Almighty; the One True God; Father; Creator; A Mighty Fortress; Provider; Friend.

16

Get that Paddle Ready, The Time has Come!

It is finally time to let the bidding begin…in preparation for this momentous event some of you may have thought would never come, please consider with me all the wonders you have experienced on this day.

We began with the entrance to an area of the auction house that was filled to overflowing with everything God knew you would need throughout your lifetime – Do you remember your excitement in that Roomful of Miracles collected specifically for you, that collection of beauty, joy, protection, and needed areas of wisdom?

Do you remember your introduction to the Auctioneer? Do you suppose there were others waiting outside the door hoping for another opportunity to again hear His stories preparing you for life? But, on this day, you were the one close enough to feel the warmth of His smile. Oh such Love…

And, then the time spent in the presence of the Owner of

the Auction House! Words can scarcely describe…especially the eyes that looked upon you with such love. You will never forget the joy in your soul as the Owner of the Auction House, God, told you just how much He treasures you. A truly momentous and life-changing experience!

Then came your need for a PLAN to navigate what is needed today and what must wait because God knows the time is not quite right. Your decision to negotiate nothing with regards to your belief in and love for Him has given you strength and understanding already.

Where else could all of this day lead but to gratitude? Choosing to let God be God; letting yourself be grateful for all the grace and mercy and love offered.

Those times of genuine joy then led to moments of truly knowing yourself, an awareness of how easily human beings want to manipulate reality with the words "If" and "If Only." Add to that a few suggestions for becoming the person God intended for you to be, and it became evident that God has a plan for your life that could never be possible on your own. God desires your life to be one of purpose and wants your life to have a grace-filled impact on this world; He trusts you, and He loves you!

———•———

May I remind you of explanations given upon your arrival this morning?

The bid for each glorious item is the following: your life – not the loss of your life but the exchange of elements you already have: your trust, your faith, your pride, your time, your love, all given in exchange for gifts greater than you can imagine! Please note two very important facts: your trust and your faith will be considered payment "As Is." You will not be perfect; you may not fully understand all there is to learn about God and Jesus and life, but who you are at this moment, and based on your choice to accept Jesus as Savior and Lord is all you need for this auction.

**Your "As Is" is a treasure recognized
and a promise for the future.
God will do the polishing as you grow.**

Each and every item is yours for the asking. It only requires your **choice** to accept each offering, to enjoy, to treasure, to recognize the value of each one. The price has already been paid – your presence is all the Auctioneer is waiting for.

A bid in this setting is no gamble, no bet in a poker game, no sacrifice any greater than the one already made by the Auctioneer. His name is Jesus, and He has been waiting for your arrival!

His Father, the Owner of the Auction House, has considered carefully all the items and reserved this special section just for you. That area is for a private auction – it was created and filled with treasure just for you. It may contain something others cannot see; it may contain a few surprises, because the items have been uniquely collected to guide you on your journey throughout life. This special collection contains all you will ever need, all you will ever truly want, and all the wonderful gifts God has in store for you – many of which you have never dreamed of!

As you again walk among the items, you are filled with wonder and anticipation; your heart and your mind begin to realize that this time you have the opportunity to realize your dreams, your desires and your need to live a life worthy of God's calling! This time there is no doubt that all will not be selected, because you are not quite ready. This time there is a greater understanding. This time you know that your greatest treasure is time with God and gratitude for Jesus. This time you begin to look more closely at the items and make wiser choices than you might have this morning.

I am so glad you noticed the word "Wisdom" standing a little higher than the rest. Perhaps you decide that is a good first selection, to carry with you in case you are in need of a reminder as you walk. Proverbs 9:10 ESV says, "The fear of the Lord is the beginning of wisdom and the knowledge of the Holy One is insight."

As you raise that Paddle high, your next "exchange" leads you to the word Faith. And then there is Grace; you wrap both in your arms and move forward keeping in mind the words of II Corinthians 6:1 ESV, "we appeal to you not to receive the grace of God in vain."

To your right is another table filled with objects designed to remind you of God's blessings:

…a Shepherd's Crook to lead your soul as David wrote in Psalm 23. You now understand that the rod and staff mentioned are not to harm you but to teach and guide you. You even smile as a bottle of allergy pills have been included for your day in "green pastures."

…walking shoes for taking the Gospel of Peace to others.

…Are you surprised to see "Right Turn Only" signs?

Let me explain: I had the privilege of leading Junior Achievement for my grandson, Colton's 2nd grade classroom last year. As the day went on and students were to choose one of two options hidden in my closed hands, I began to see a pattern. When I asked them why they always chose the right hand for their desired answer the unanimous response given loudly was, "Right is always the right choice." As I looked back over the day, I realized I had unconsciously put the correct answer in my right hand every time, even when I put both hands behind my back and shifted the objects while focusing on the discussion occurring. Right is always Right, thus those "Right Turn Only signs" can always serve as a reminder in times of temptation. Grab those too – one for home, for work, one for the dashboard of your car.

There is a map; therefore, you need a compass. A Welcoming sign to the Path you are to follow when seeking truth and love and compassion and God's Will is a definite Must!

Key chains reminding you of the temptation of feeling you must try to access God's goodness on your own – it will be a reminder to simply ask Him. That keychain has another purpose as well – the Bible is your key to knowledge and understanding. Your prayers are the key to building a close and personal relationship with the One who seeks your friendship as well.

Goodness and Mercy toward others would be good addition to your armful, too. Never forget that God's goodness and mercy are not only undeserved gifts, but they are examples you must follow in your relationships with family, with friends, co-workers and those who are struggling.

The flashlight already has your name engraved on it! God will never be hard to find. And, you will never be lost with the Holy Spirit by your side. He will gently nudge you when tempted to take a left turn rather than a right turn. He will grant you understanding in those moments you are uncertain how to respond, or what choice is needing to be made. He can even warn you of the hole in the sidewalk ahead.

Knee pads for your prayer time and for the 'work' you will be doing for the Lord.

The next items seem little confusing: ear plugs *and* earphones? Yes, you are correct - ear plugs for the many times you will need to turn off the temptations of the world. Evil will call your name and seek to entice you into sin relentlessly. God's specially designed ear plugs will block out evil's attempts to mislead you but never block out Jesus' loving forgiveness and God's love and guidance. (Did you catch that? Both are sending love your way!) Next, pick up those earphones that insure you can always hear the beautiful music of the Heaven in times you are seeking peace and joy. Hear the gospel and the voices of those sent to teach you more from your Bible.

Speaking of your Bible, are you in need of an extra pair of glasses? Yes, there are large print Bibles, but sometimes you will just want to 'read' between the lines to see the love that goes into every word God has provided to teach, encourage, prepare, and love you.

Do not; Do not; Do not miss the Bible in the center of this table. It is the Owner's Manual for human beings to navigate, repair, and enjoy this life as you know it. Have your tools ready for life-long responsibilities. Hold that Bible close to your chest, in gratitude! And more! Recognize that 316 on the Paddle used as your bid represents the best verse in your Bible. "For God so loved the world that He gave His only begotten Son, that whosoever believeth in him should not perish, but have everlasting life" John 3:17 NIV.

One last item I do want you to take with you. It is a "closet" for your prayer times. In opening the door you may see beautiful sunrises and sunsets; you may see hospital rooms; you may see children's faces filled with utter joy. Or you may see tears – your tears or tears of others. This wonderful prayer closet will remind you that God is everywhere, waiting just for your prayers of honesty and love, at any and all times. But, is has to be your choice to enter into the times of prayer. Don't close the door; instead, leave it open as you navigate the rest of your room in the Auction House. Let your prayers express gratitude and beg for wisdom and exhibit faith as you walk. Reach just inside that door of your personal prayer closet and take hold of the hand of One who seeks to guide you now and through the rest of your life.

So much to see; So many blessings! While I could continue to describe every item you might see, I ask you to spend time in prayer and reading your Bible. Those are God's conversations with you. Conversations not to be missed.

However, there are two tables I want to direct you to before we go. One is the Banquet Table always set for Supper with the Lord, and you are always invited. Always. It is glorious and ready for the celebrations that will occur throughout your lifetime. It is also where you may come anytime you need to feel close to today's Auctioneer and Owner, not to mention your Guide throughout this visit.

**You need to celebrate them; they need
to celebrate you, in person.
Make time for that regardless of
the pressures of your day.**

The other table is one of Encouragement in times of hurt and difficulty and confusion and loss. It is one where you are not required to put your best foot forward or maintain that stiff upper lip. That table is for honest conversation; heads may be hung low or tempers may even flare. But that table of Encouragement is provided to graciously give you the comfort, the understanding, the love and wisdom needed so badly. And, as always, God will be at the head of the table welcoming you and helping you see a way through hard times. That table is already worn and perhaps the china and crystal have a few chips. Remember that is the place for honest conversation. Never fail to see that your Name Card is engraved in gold as you arrive. God knows when you need to be there, and He is always prepared to welcome you. One important fact: The doors of this particular Auction House never close. The Owner, Auctioneer and Guide are always looking forward to your visits.

All you must do is choose to participate in the auction of a lifetime. Choose to be blessed; to be forgiven; to be protected; to be loved, and to be amazed by the quality, joy and peace of each item offered. Choose to give up your old "trade-in" that is battered, broken, imperfect, and weak for that which IS perfect and perfectly given by the God of the Universe.